The Allgemeine-SS

Robin Lumsden • Illustrated by Paul Hannon

Series editor Martin Windrow

First published in Great Britain in 1993 by
Osprey Publishing, Elms Court, Chapel Way, Botley,
Oxford OX2 9LP, United Kingdom.
Email: info@ospreypublishing.com

©1993 Osprey Publishing Ltd.
Reprinted 1994, 1996, 1997, 1999, 2001, 2002, 2003, 2004

CIP Data for this publication is available from
the British Library

ISBN 1 85532 358 3

Series Editor: MARTIN WINDROW

Filmset in Great Britain
Printed in China through World Print Ltd.

FOR A CATALOGUE OF ALL BOOKS PUBLISHED BY
OSPREY MILITARY AND AVIATION PLEASE CONTACT:

The Marketing Manager, Osprey Direct UK,
PO Box 140, Wellingborough, Northants,
NN8 2FA, United Kingdom.
Email: info@ospreydirect.co.uk

The Marketing Manager, Osprey Direct USA,
c/o MBI Publishing, PO Box 1,
729 Prospect Avenue, Osceola, WI 54020, USA.
Email: info@ospreydirectusa.com

www.ospreypublishing.com

Author's acknowledgements:
I wish to express my sincere appreciation to the
following individuals, for their assistance in supplying
me with much needed documentary and illustrative
material: Robert Hoffmann, Munich; Dr. David
Marwell, Berlin; Oberstleutnant Heinrich Paprotka,
Rastatt; and Reinhard Puchelski, Berlin.

Photographs credited 'IWM' are reproduced by
kind permission of the Trustees of the Imperial War
Museum, London, while the pictures of surviving
examples of SS regalia from my own collection were
taken by Alan Lauder of Norval Ltd., Dunfermline.

Last, but by no means least, a heartfelt word of
thanks goes to Iain Lumsden, whose suggestions one
Sunday afternoon resulted in this book being written.

THE ALLGEMEINE-SS

INTRODUCTION

The SS, an offshoot of the SA (see MAA 220), originated as Hitler's personal bodyguard, and after the Nazi consolidation of power in 1933 began to develop rapidly. Firstly, the bodyguard section grew to regimental strength and became the elite unit of the entire organisation, assuming the title Leibstandarte-SS 'Adolf Hitler'. Secondly, the SS-Verfügungstruppe were formed as barracked quasi-military forces to bolster the new regime in the event of political turmoil or counter-revolution. Finally, the SS-Totenkopfverbände were recruited to guard the growing number of concentration camp inmates. These three groupings of the SS were amalgamated to a certain extent during the war, becoming the first three divisions of the Waffen-SS (see MAA 34), which expanded as a fourth branch of the Wehrmacht to encompass almost 40 field divisions by 1945.

The purpose of this book is to cover, briefly, the history, organisation and uniforms of the rest of the SS: those men and women who came to be known by the blanket (and somewhat disparaging) term Allgemeine-SS, or 'General SS'. Some had tried, and failed, to gain entry to the Leibstandarte, Verfügungstruppe or Totenkopfverbände. Others, for whatever personal or domestic reasons, chose to remain with the largely part-time and usually unpaid local units. In any event, while the more visible armed SS combat units naturally received all the publicity, especially during the war, it was the rather faceless Allgemeine-SS which wielded the real power.

Its membership included the entire spectrum of the German civil population, from farm labourers to the landed aristocracy and from small shopkeepers to the directors of national companies. Its academics engaged upon research projects and intelligence-gathering activities which had a great influence on both the domestic and foreign policies of the Third Reich. The government, industry, commerce, educ-

The Stosstrupp Adolf Hitler, 2 September 1923. Josef Berchtold, the unit commander, stands leaning on the cab, beside the Imperial War Flag. Uniforms are of the field-grey Reichswehr type, with NSDAP armbands and death's heads.

ation, and particularly the police all came to be dominated by the Allgemeine-SS. In occupied western Europe local volunteer units, known as the Germanic-SS, were set up in Flanders, Holland, Norway and Denmark to support the local police in guarding the various Home Fronts. By 1943 the Allgemeine-SS had evolved from a part-time provincial police reserve to a force which influenced, through its highly placed members, much of the political, racial, cultural and economic face of Europe. Its total active strength was at that stage less than 40,000 because of the demands of military conscription; yet it successfully operated across an area stretching from the Channel Islands to the Black Sea and from the Arctic Circle to the Mediterranean—an area with a generally hostile population. Right up until the collapse of the Nazi regime the tentacles of the Allgemeine-SS retained a firm grip on all aspects of life in the Third Reich.

EARLY HISTORY

At the end of 1918, nationalist groups sprang up all over Germany with the aim of ridding the country of

demobilised right-wing troops who had banded together on a voluntary basis to smash riots, keep order in the streets, and prevent Germany from becoming a Bolshevik regime. Freikorps leaders like Ernst Röhm sent Hitler a constant stream of officers, NCOs and men; and in October 1920 the veterans of the Ehrhardt Brigade and the Iron Division went over en masse to the new party, taking with them their swastika and death's head badges.

The military nature of the NSDAP grew with the setting up of the Sturmabteilung or SA during 1921. This was the work of Röhm and the ex-naval Leutnant Hans-Ulrich Klintzsch, who created the SA as a new Freikorps to hammer the Reds and fend off opponents at political meetings. However, although the SA was affiliated to the party, it did not initially come under Hitler's personal authority, for its members had little respect for the finesse of politics. By the time it paraded before Hitler at the first national rally of the NSDAP in January 1923 the SA numbered 6,000 men in four regiments, and there were sufficient recruits during the next month alone to form a fifth. In an effort to improve control over the rapidly growing organisation Hitler appointed a new man of politics, Hermann Göring, to lead it; but he was by nature lazy and self-indulgent, and the true driving force behind the SA remained Röhm. Frustrated by Röhm's ambition and independence, which were upheld by the former leaders of the Freikorps, Hitler was compelled to set up a small troop of men from outside the SA which would be entirely devoted to him. Thus the SS was born.

Men of the newly formed SS proudly display an NSDAP Feldzeichen, 1925. Note varieties of dress, particularly the short-lived 'Krätzchen' field caps with massive eagle insignia and the assorted belt buckles.*

the 'November Traitors' who had brought the disgrace of the dictated peace at Versailles, and of the Communists and Spartacists whose first loyalty was to Russia. Nationalists came from every level of society; and at the lower end of the Munich social scale was Anton Drexler's tiny German Workers' Party, one of whose meetings Adolf Hitler attended as a military observer in September 1919. He joined the party and, through his powers of oratory, virtually took it over from the outset, changing its name to the National Socialist German Workers' Party (Nationalsozialistische Deutsche Arbeiterpartei, or NSDAP).

Hitler's speeches soon found a loud echo in the ranks of the Freikorps, the hastily formed units of

The Munich Putsch

In March 1923 Hitler ordered the formation of the Munich-based bodyguard known as the Stabswache, whose members swore an oath of loyalty to him personally. Two months later, to avoid confusion with an SA unit of the same name which protected Röhm and Göring, the Stabswache was renamed the Stosstrupp Adolf Hitler and, like the German army shock troops of World War I, it adopted the death's head as its distinctive emblem. The Stosstrupp Hitler was led by Julius Schreck and Josef Berchtold, and its membership included Josef 'Sepp' Dietrich, Rudolf Hess, Julius Schaub, Ulrich Graf and Karl Fiehler. The 30-man squad participated in the ill-fated Munich Putsch on 9 November 1923, when Hitler's attempt to seize power in Bavaria by force ended in disaster. During the episode Graf saved the Führer's life, so fulfilling the primary duty of the Stosstrupp. He was later rewarded with the title 'des Führers alter Begleiter', or 'The Führer's Senior Bodyguard', and his bravery that day left a lasting impression on Hitler.

Following the Putsch the NSDAP was banned and the SA dissolved. On his release from prison in December 1924 Hitler began to rebuild his party, and now categorically forbade the SA to bear arms or function as any form of private army. Its purpose was solely to clear the streets of his political enemies—a role hotly contested by Röhm, who always envisaged the SA as a citizen army which would ultimately supersede the Reichswehr. The disagreements between the two became so bitter that Röhm eventually resigned from the NSDAP and quit Germany for a military advisor's post in Bolivia; however, his absence had such an impact that Hitler was subsequently forced to reinstate him as SA chief in a stronger position than ever.

In April 1925 Hitler formed a new bodyguard commanded by Schaub, Schreck and his other Stosstrupp favourites. The guard, which came under the auspices of the SA High Command, was known first as the Schutzkommando, then as the Sturmstaffel; but on 9 November it adopted the title of Schutzstaffel or Protection Squad, soon commonly abbreviated to SS. From the start it was laid down that the SS, unlike the SA, should never become a mass organisation. Groups of Ten, or 'Zehnerstaffeln', were set up across Germany so that the Führer could have access to a local SS bodyguard wherever he went during his political campaigning. Applicants had to be between 25 and 35 years of age, have two sponsors, be registered with the police as residents of five years' standing, and be sober, disciplined, strong and healthy. The seeds of elitism were sown.

Despite the gradual extension of its numbers and prestige, the SS remained a limited organisation subordinated to the SA. The latter kept a jealous eye on SS expansion, and local SA commanders consistently used the SS under their control for the most demeaning tasks such as distributing propaganda leaflets and recruiting subscribers to the party newspaper, the 'Völkischer Beobachter'. By the end of 1928 morale in the SS was at an all-time low.

Himmler takes control

The watershed in the development of the SS can be traced to a single date—6 January 1929. On that fateful day Heinrich Himmler took command of the organisation at a time when the SA was becoming increasingly rebellious. From then on SS progress became bound up with the career of Himmler, who obtained one important post after another; indeed, by 1945 he had concentrated more power in his hands than any other man except Hitler. In April 1929 Himmler obtained approval for a recruiting plan designed to create a truly elite body out of the SS; and by 1930 it had grown to a force of 2,000 men. When the SA in northern Germany rebelled against the bourgeois NSDAP hierarchy in 1931, only the SS remained loyal to Hitler. The revolt collapsed, and Himmler was rewarded with his appointment as security chief of the NSDAP headquarters in Munich. In effect, he was made head of the party police.

SS men prepare to set fire to a collection of placards and flags seized from Berlin Communists, March 1933. The early black uniforms reveal slight differences in cut and position of buttons, and shoulder straps have not yet been introduced. (IWM)

◀ A detachment from an SS Fuss-Standarte, preceded by its band and traditional musicians' Schellenbaum or 'Belltree' standard, c.1934.

▶ Allgemeine-SS NCO's/man's peaked cap. The 1929-pattern eagle and 1934-pattern Totenkopf date this example to c. 1935. The larger SS-style eagle was introduced in the following year. (Lumsden Collection)

On 30 January 1933 Hitler became Chancellor of Germany. Less than a month later the Reichstag building was burned to the ground, and the blame put on the Communists. Hitler immediately gave police powers to 25,000 SA and 15,000 SS men, who began to arrest left-wing opponents of the new regime in large numbers and herd them into makeshift prisons and camps. While the SS was consolidating its position and controlling its membership and recruitment by a constant purging process, the SA began to throw its weight about noisily. Denied a position in the Nazi State to which it felt entitled, the SA talked of a 'Second Revolution' which would sweep away both the bourgeois in the party and the reactionaries in the Reichswehr. The brawling, drinking, violence and homosexual activities of the SA became an embarrassment; and on 30 June 1934 the SA leadership was liquidated in operations carried out ruthlessly by the SS and the army. With Röhm dead, the SA suffered a loss of power and 'face' from which it never fully recovered.

On 20 July 1934, in thanks for its services during the 'Night of the Long Knives', Hitler declared the 200,000-strong SS an independent formation of the NSDAP and removed it completely from SA control. Its ascendancy was now assured; and it entered a period of consolidation during which it developed a new command structure and organisation under Himmler, whose rank as Reichsführer-SS for the first time actually meant what it implied and made him directly subordinate to Hitler. From the middle of 1934 the traditional non-military SS, the backbone of the organisation, began to be known as the Allgemeine-SS to distinguish it from the newly developing armed branches.

ROLE OF THE SS

The first and foremost duty of the SS was the protection of Adolf Hitler. After the advent of the Leibstandarte, however, whose members worked full-time to a rota and accompanied Hitler on his journeys through the Reich, the part-time SS men who had originally been recruited on a local basis to protect the Führer during his trips around Germany found that aspect of their work taken from them. Consequently, it was decided that as of 1934 the main day-to-day function of these highly disciplined Allgemeine-SS volunteers would be to support the police in maintaining public order.

The SS rapidly expanded with the formation of many new Allgemeine-SS Standarten, trained and equipped to combat any internal uprising or counter-revolution. In such an event the SS would take over the operation of the post office, national radio network, public utilities and public transport, as well as acting as police reinforcements. The anticipated

civil unrest never came about, and so the police duties of the Allgemeine-SS before the outbreak of war in 1939 were generally restricted to overseeing crowd control at party rallies and other celebrations, including national holidays and state visits of foreign dignitaries.

During World War II members of the Allgemeine-SS who had not been called up for military service took an active role in the war effort at home. In many cities special SS Wachkompanie and Alarmstürme were detailed to protect factories, bridges, roads and other strategic points, and to assist the Luftschutz or Civil Defence during air raids. On the Reich's borders, SS men worked as Auxiliary Frontier Personnel in conjunction with the Customs Service. Others helped with the harvest, supervised foreign labourers, and engaged upon welfare work. During 1944–45 the cadres of the Allgemeine-SS throughout Germany were trained to co-ordinate the short-lived guerrilla fighting which took place against Allied troops.

Conditions of service in the SS highlighted the elite nature of the formation. Recruiting was tightly controlled, most young SS men after 1934 coming directly from the ranks of the Hitler Youth. Out of every 100 applicants, only 10 to 15 were finally admitted. Selection was based on racial purity, good health and disciplined character. Training was carried out over a three-year period, with statutory breaks for obligatory service in the armed forces and in the Labour Service. The confirmed SS man remained in the active Allgemeine-SS until he was 35 years old, after which he could transfer to one of the SS reserve units. Promotion was awarded on merit, and a strict SS Legal Code and Discipline Code governed the behaviour of every SS member. Ultimately, SS men were answerable only to special SS and Police courts for any crimes or offences they committed, and were, in effect, put above the normal jurisdiction of the civil courts.

Under Himmler, the SS came to regard itself not merely as a temporary political organisation but as a 'Sippe', i.e. a tribe or clan. The same racial qualities looked for in the SS man were therefore also required of his wife. A special Marriage Order, dating from 1931, dictated that SS men had to seek permission to marry, and that the prospective wives had to undergo close scrutiny into their health, background and fertility. Christian weddings were replaced by neo-pagan rites for the Allgemeine-SS, and couples were expected to raise at least four children, either naturally or by adoption. A network of maternity homes administered by the SS Lebensborn Society was set up to assist in that goal.

The SS in Germany

The Allgemeine-SS had a wide-ranging effect on all aspects of life in Nazi Germany. The racial policies of the Third Reich were put into operation through SS agencies, primarily the Reichskommissariat für die Festigung des deutschen Volkstums or RKFDV, the Reich Commission for the Consolidation of Germanism, which organised the resettlement of racial Germans in the occupied eastern territories. Another SS group, the Volksdeutsche Mittelstelle or VOMI, played a significant part in infiltrating racial German communities in Austria and Czechoslovakia during the late 1930s, ultimately paving the way for the Nazi occupation of these states. In an effort to prove the racial hypotheses of National Socialism by scientific means Himmler set up Ahnenerbe, a body for the research of ancestral heritage. The SS duly carried out archaeological excavations throughout Europe in the search for the origins of the Nordic race—an apparently innocent obsession which ultimately resulted in human experimentation using concentration camp inmates.

The concentration camp system also gave the SS access to an unlimited supply of cheap, expendable labour, which led to a thriving SS economy. Various manufacturing enterprises were set up in the camps, and workers leased out to private firms on subcontract. The acquisition of large fertile territories during the war greatly enlarged the scope of these activities. Farming and stockbreeding in Poland, and forestry, mining and fishing in Russia all entered the field of SS economics, and between 1941 and 1944 the SS exploited the wealth, resources and population of the conquered east on a massive scale. Himmler eventually controlled over 500 factories, producing, for example, 75% of Germany's soft drinks and 95% of the country's furniture. Most of the uniforms and equipment used by the Allgemeine-SS, Waffen-SS and police were manufactured in the concentration camps, alongside military armaments and leather goods. The SS ran quarries, brickworks, cement factories, bakeries, food research establishments and processing plants, a publishing house, a sword smithy and even a porcelain works. The sums which flowed into SS coffers as a result were vast, and helped to strengthen the Reichsführer's position and maintain the financial autonomy of his organisation.

Through its industrial connections, the SS cultivated and recruited hundreds of company directors, businessmen and landowners. Many of these influential men became members of the Circle of Friends of the Reichsführer-SS, or SS Patron Members, and made regular donations to SS funds. In return, they secured the protection and favour of the Black Corps. By means of a conscious policy of infiltration, the SS thoroughly permeated every branch of official and semi-official German life. By May 1944 no less than 25% of the leading personalities in Germany were members of the SS, some being regulars and others so-called 'Ehrenführer' or Honorary Officers. They included almost all of Hitler's immediate entourage, men in key party and government posts, top civil servants, the leaders of local govenment, members of the military aristocracy, doctors, scientists and those prominent in the fields of culture and charitable works. After the failed plot to assassinate Hitler in July 1944 the SS finally overcame the last bastion of the old traditional Germany, the army; SS generals took over the Home Army and military administration, as well as the secret weapons programme.

With its eyes clearly set on the future, the SS set out to control the education system at an early stage and with considerable success. The NPEA schools, which existed to train the future elite of the party, fell under SS direction, as did the Students' League and the Teachers' Association. Above all, the Hitler Youth worked hand-in-glove with the SS so that the racial and political thinking of the NSDAP could be transmitted to the young. Many of the uniform accoutrements and rituals of the Hitler Youth were copied directly from those of the SS.

By the autumn of 1944, the SS had seized almost total political, military and economic control of Germany. At the beginning of 1945, however, Himmler failed in his post as military commander of two Army Groups on the Rhine and Vistula Fronts, and even sought to negotiate a peace treaty with the Western Allies. Hitler dismissed him, replacing him as Reichsführer-SS by Karl Hanke. With the Führer's suicide on 30 April the Third Reich rapidly collapsed; and all factions of the Nazi regime were only too happy to heap the blame for their atrocities on the shoulders of the SS. The entire organisation was declared criminal by the victors, and its members hunted down. Himmler and several of his generals took their own lives rather than face the ordeal of a trial and a certain death sentence. Lesser SS officers, NCOs and men simply melted into the background of post-war Germany, or fled abroad with the assistance of the secret ODESSA organisation. Some used part of the estimated £900,000,000 worth of money and assets held by the SS in 1945 to establish commercial companies throughout the world, many of which are still in existence to this day.

Himmler placing a wreath at the Feldherrnhalle, 9 November 1934. The Blood Banner, held by Jakob Grimminger, stands in the background. The Reichsführer wears one of his favoured leather overcoats. The guard of honour comprises members of the SS-VT, still dressed in black.

ORGANISATION

The command structure of the Allgemeine-SS continually grew and developed during the 1930s. By 1942, subject to Himmler's controlling authority and that of his High Command the Reichsführung-SS, the day-to-day work of directing and administering the SS was carried out by eight main departments, or Hauptämter, as listed below.

Hauptamt Persönlicher Stab RfSS (Pers. Stab RfSS)
This was Himmler's personal staff and comprised the heads of the SS Hauptämter, certain specialist officials, and advisory or honorary officers. Its administrative work was processed through the Kommandostab RfSS, which operated during the war under the title Feldkommandostelle RfSS or Field Headquarters of the Reichsführer-SS. It was then organised like a military HQ, with a signals section, escort battalion and flak detachment, and accompanied Himmler on his tours of the occupied territories.

SS Hauptamt (SS-HA)
The SS Central Office was mainly responsible for recruitment and the maintenance of records on non-commissioned personnel.

SS Führungshauptamt (SS-FHA)
The SS Operational Headquarters included as one of its main departments the Kommandoamt der Allgemeinen-SS, or Allgemeine-SS HQ, and co-ordinated training, the payment of wages, the supply of equipment, arms, ammunition and vehicles and the maintenance and repair of stocks. It was also responsible for the transport of the SS and Police, SS mail censorship, geology, war archives and dental and medical services.

Reichssicherheitshauptamt (RSHA or RSi-H)
The Reich Central Security Office controlled the Security Agencies of the Third Reich, including the Kripo, the Gestapo and the SD. It was responsible for both foreign and domestic intelligence operations, espionage and counter-espionage, combatting political and common law crime, and sounding out public opinion on the Nazi regime.

SS Wirtschafts- und Verwaltungshauptamt (SS-WVHA)
The SS Economic and Administrative Department controlled a large number of SS industrial and agricultural undertakings, carried out housing and construction programmes, administered the finances of the SS and ran the concentration camps.

Rasse- und Siedlungshauptamt (RuSHA)
The Race and Settlement Department looked after the racial purity of all SS members, issued lineage certificates, and was responsible for settling SS men, especially ex-servicemen, in the conquered eastern territories.

Hauptamt SS-Gericht (HA SS-Gericht)
The SS Legal Department administered the disciplinary side of the special code of laws to which members of the SS and police were subject. It controlled the SS and Police courts, and the penal camps to which convicted SS and police offenders were sent.

SS Personalhauptamt (Pers.HA)
The SS Personnel Department dealt with personnel matters and kept records on SS officers.

Regional organisation

On a level immediately below the SS Hauptämter were the Oberabschnitte (Oa.) or Regions, the bases of the Allgemeine-SS territorial organisation. Initially there were five Oberabschnitte, formed in 1932 from the existing SS Gruppen. By 1944 their number had risen to 17 within Germany proper, and each corresponded almost exactly to a Wehrkreis or Military District. The SS Regions were generally known by geographical names, but it was also

Copy of the newspaper 'Das Schwarze Korps' published weekly by the SS high command to keep members up to date on SS affairs. (Lumsden Collection)

customary to refer to them by the Roman numeral allocated to the corresponding Wehrkreis. In addition, six foreign Oberabschnitte evolved during the war in the occupied territories.

Each Oberabschnitt was commanded by an SS-Obergruppenführer, Gruppenführer or Brigadeführer designated Führer des Oberabschnittes (F.Oa.). He was usually also Himmler's representative at the military HQ of the local Wehrkreis and, in addition, held the post of Höhere SS- und Polizeiführer or HSSPf, the Senior SS and Police Commander in the Region. The Regional SS Headquarters was staffed by full-time officers, assisted by a number of voluntary part-time officials.

Every SS Oberabschnitt in turn comprised an average of three Abschnitte or Districts, again distinguished by Roman numerals. They were also referred to by the name of the area they covered, or by the location of their headquarters. The Abschnitt commander, or Führer des Abschnittes (F.Ab.) was generally an officer of the rank of SS-Oberführer or Standartenführer. By 1944 there were 45 Abschnitte, with some large towns and cities being split between two of them.

Unit organisation

The organisation of the Allgemeine-SS below the level of the Abschnitt was on a unit rather than territorial basis to increase flexibility, although each

This table shows the typical breakdown of units within an Allgemeine-SS Oberabschnitt, using Oberabschnitt Fulda-Werra as an example. (Reproduced from 'The General SS', produced by Allied Counter-Intelligence in 1944)

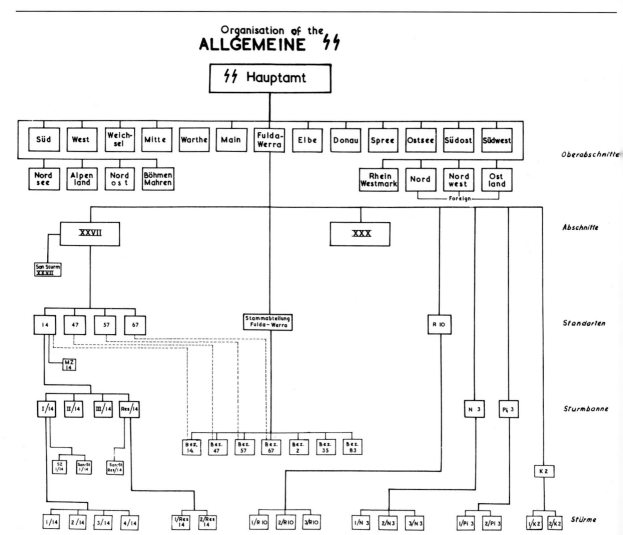

SS Ranks until 1942

Although the SS became one of the most complex of all the Nazi paramilitary organisations, its rank structure remained relatively stable and underwent few major alterations. The nine initial ranks employed by the SS, based on those of the SA, were:

SS-Mann
SS-Scharführer
SS-Truppführer
SS-Sturmführer
SS-Sturmbannführer
SS-Standartenführer
SS-Oberführer
SS-Gruppenführer
SS-Obergruppenführer

On 19 May 1933, a further eight ranks were created to accommodate the general expansion of the SS, namely:

SS-Sturmmann
SS-Rottenführer
SS-Oberscharführer
SS-Obertruppführer
SS-Obersturmführer
SS-Sturmhauptführer
SS-Obersturmbannführer
SS-Brigadeführer

In August 1934, Himmler was elevated to the new rank of Reichsführer-SS and given insignia unique to his position, replacing the SS-Obergruppenführer badges he wore prior to that time.

On 15 October 1934, further revisions were made to the SS rank system, as indicated below:
SS-Bewerber was added as the lowest rank
SS-Anwärter was added as the second lowest rank
SS-Scharführer became SS-Unterscharführer
SS-Oberscharführer became SS-Scharführer
SS-Truppführer became SS-Oberscharführer
SS-Obertruppführer became SS-Hauptscharführer
SS-Sturmführer became SS-Untersturmführer
SS-Sturmhauptführer became SS-Hauptsturmführer

Rank insignia remained unchanged from that point until 7 April 1942, when new collar patches were introduced for:
SS-Oberführer
SS-Brigadeführer
SS-Gruppenführer
SS-Obergruppenführer
At the same time a new and senior rank of SS-Oberst-Gruppenführer was created.

SS Ranks April 1942–May 1945

The final Allgemeine-SS rank structure, dating from April 1942 was as follows:

Mannschaften (Other Ranks)

SS-Bewerber	Candidate
SS-Anwärter	Cadet
SS-Mann	Private
SS-Sturmmann (Strm.)	Lance Corporal
SS-Rottenführer (Rotf.)	Senior Lance Corporal

Unterführer (NCOs)

SS-Unterscharführer (Uschaf.)	Corporal
SS-Scharführer (Schaf.)	Sergeant
SS-Oberscharführer (Oschaf.)	Staff Sergeant
SS-Hauptscharführer (Hschaf.)	Sergeant-Major

Untere Führer (Junior Officers)

SS-Untersturmführer (Ustuf.)	2nd Lieutenant
SS-Obersturmführer (Ostuf.)	Lieutenant
SS-Hauptsturmführer (Hstuf.)	Captain

Mittlere Führer (Intermediate Officers)

SS-Sturmbannführer (Stubaf.)	Major
SS-Obersturmbannführer (Ostubaf.)	Lt. Colonel

Höhere Führer (Senior Officers)

SS-Standartenführer (Staf.)	Colonel
SS-Oberführer (Oberf.)	Senior Colonel
SS-Brigadeführer (Brif.)	Brigadier
SS-Gruppenführer (Gruf.)	Major-General
SS-Obergruppenführer (Ogruf.)	Lt. General
SS-Oberst-Gruppenführer (Obstgruf.)	General
Reichsführer-SS (RfSS)	Supreme Commander

Hitler himself was ultimately Commander-in-Chief of the SS and held the personal title of 'Der Oberste Führer der Schutzstaffel'.

unit was related to, or recruited from, a particular area.

The typical Abschnitt controlled an average of three SS Fuss-Standarten, the equivalent of foot or infantry regiments. As the name suggests, the Standarte was the standard unit of the Allgemeine-SS and had been firmly established as such by 1929, long before the SS Regional system fully evolved. Prior to the war the average Fuss-Standarte comprised around 2,000 men, but numbers fell to around 1,600 in 1941, and as low as 400 in 1944, due to Allgemeine-SS members being drafted into the Wehrmacht and Waffen-SS. Each regiment was commanded by a Führer des Standartes (F.Sta.) who was assisted by a small staff and part-time HQ unit. Depending on unit size, the regimental commander could be an SS-Standartenführer, Obersturmbannführer or Sturmbannführer. By 1943 it was common for two of the smaller adjacent Standarten to be placed together under a single acting commander. Standarten were numbered consecutively from 1 to 126. A select few

also bore the names of celebrated SS men who had died or been killed, and such honour titles were similarly extended to a number of Stürme within certain Standarten.

As well as the Fuss-Standarten, there were 22 Allgemeine-SS cavalry units of regimental size, the Reiterstandarten. Each comprised from five to eight Reiterstürme (cavalry companies), a Sanitätsreiterstaffel (cavalry medical squad) and a Trompeterkorps (trumpet corps). The Reiterstandarten were never concentrated in their HQ city, the component companies usually being dispersed amongst smaller towns of the Abschnitte. They were always essentially ceremonial in function, and were seldom if ever used to assist the Fuss-Standarten and Police in domestic crowd control. The SS Reiterstandarten were numbered from 1 to 22, each number being prefixed by the letter 'R' to distinguish them from the foot regiments. Many of their headquarters were sited in former garrison towns of Imperial cavalry units, with excellent equestrian facilities. After the outbreak of war in 1939 the majority of members of the Reiterstandarten were conscripted into army cavalry units, or into the hastily mustered SS-Totenkopfreiterstandarten for front-line service. In 1941 the latter amalgamated to form the Waffen-SS Cavalry Brigade which by 1942 had expanded to become the SS-Kavallerie-Division, named 'Florian Geyer' in 1944.

Each SS Standarte was composed of three active Sturmbanne or battalions, one Reserve-Sturmbann for men between the ages of 35 and 45, and a Musikzug or marching band. A Sturmbann was usually commanded by an SS-Sturmbannführer, assisted by an adjutant. The full peacetime strength of a Sturmbann ranged from 500 to 800 men and, since it was considered the basic tactical unit of the Allgemeine-SS, it was planned that the SS Sturmbann would be able to operate as an independent

Rangabzeichen der S.=A. und S.=S.
auf dem linken Kragenspiegel

S.=A.=Mann — Sturmmann — Rottenführer

Scharführer — Oberscharführer — Truppführer

Obertruppführer San.=Sturmbannarzt-Anwärter — Sturmführer San.=Sturmführer — Obersturmführer San.=Obersturmführer

Sturmhauptführer San.=Sturmhauptführer — Sturmbannführer San.=Sturmbannführer — Obersturmbannführer San.=Obersturmbannführer

Standartenführer San.=Standartenführer — Oberführer San.=Oberführer — Brigadeführer San.=Brigadeführer

Gruppenführer San.=Gruppenführer — Obergruppenführer San.=Obergruppenführer — Chef des Stabes

(Die Sanitäterabzeichen werden auf beiden Kragenspiegeln getragen)

Rank Badges of the SA and SS, c. May 1934.
At this stage, lower ranks had unpiped (later white piped) collar patches while junior officers' patches were piped in black and silver twisted cord and those of senior officers in plain silver. Early terms such as Sturmhauptführer *still feature, and there is no special insignia for Himmler, who, even though he held the post of Reichsführer der SS, was ranked simply as an SS-Obergruppenführer. (Reproduced from 'Die Uniformen der Braunhemden', 1934)*

entity in time of strife or revolt. The three active Sturmbanne of a Standarte were numbered in Roman numerals from I to III; e.g. the 3rd Sturmbann of the 41st Standarte was abbreviated 'III/41'. The Reserve-Sturmbann was distinguished by the prefix 'Res.', in this case 'Res./41'.

Each active Sturmbann was in turn composed of four Stürme or companies, a Sanitätsstaffel (medical squad) and a Spielmannzug (fife-and-drum corps). The full peacetime strength of a Sturm was 120 to 180 men, under an SS-Hauptsturmführer, Obersturmführer or Untersturmführer. During wartime one of the four Stürme served locally as a Wachkompanie or Guard Company protecting strategic points. Another stood by as a civil defence Alarmsturm or Emergency Company for use during air raids, and the remaining two were assigned to general patrol duties. A Reserve-Sturmbann generally comprised two Reserve-Stürme, numbered 'Res.1' and 'Res.2', and a Reserve-Sanitätsstaffel.

Within each Standarte, the four Stürme of Sturmbann I were numbered 1, 2, 3 and 4. Those of Sturmbann II were numbered 5, 6, 7 and 8 and those of Sturmbann III were numbered 9, 10, 11 and 12. Thus the 1st Sturm of the 2nd Sturmbann of the 3rd Standarte, i.e. the 5th Sturm in the 3rd Standarte, would be referred to within the Standarte as '5/II' and outside the Standarte as '5/3'.

Every Sturm was divided into three or four Truppen (platoons), each composed of three Scharen (sections). A Schar generally numbered 10 to 15 men, and was used to patrol blocks of houses within cities and guard official buildings. The Schar itself comprised two or three Rotten (files), the smallest units of the Allgemeine-SS, numbering about 5 men. Depending on their size, Truppen and Scharen were commanded by NCOs of the ranks between SS-Hauptscharführer and Unterscharführer, while Rotten were led by experienced enlisted men known as Rottenführer.

Specialist formations

Each SS Oberabschnitt was assigned one Nachrichtensturmbann or signals battalion, responsible for SS communications in the Region. These signals battalions were numbered from 1 to 19, in Arabic rather than Roman numerals, prefixed by the letters 'Na.'.

Pioniersturmbanne or engineer battalions were again organic components of the Oberabschnitte, and were equipped to carry out emergency construction work such as road and bridge repairs, and maintenance of public utilities including gas, electricity and water supplies. Each Pioniersturmbann was numbered consecutively from 1 to 16, prefixed by the letters 'Pi.'.

The Röntgensturmbann SS-HA, or SS Hauptamt X-Ray Battalion, was composed of 350 full-time SS men, and toured all the Allgemeine-SS Oberabschnitte carrying out routine health checks on SS personnel. It utilised portable X-ray equipment, and was primarily employed to detect pulmonary diseases

Specialist Officer Badges. These were worn on the left sleeve above the cuff title by specialist SS officers. From top to bottom, they denoted expertise in the following: Recruiting and Training, Race and Resettlement, Germanic Colonisation, *Racial German Assistance, Building Administration, Economic Enterprises, Agricultural Administration, Press and War Economy, SS and Police Liaison. (Reproduced from the Organisationsbuch der NSDAP, 1943 edition)*

Stand: 1943	Fachführerabzeichen — SS-Fachunterführer und SS-Fachführer	
	Dienststelle	Armelabzeichen
	SS-Hauptamt (Ergänzung, Erfassung und Schulung)	
	SS-Rasse und Siedlungshauptamt (Rasse- und Siedlungswesen)	
Reichskommissariat für die Festigung deutschen Volkstums	Stabshauptamt (Gruppe Siedlung)	
	Volksdeutschenmittelstelle (Gruppe Volkstumsarbeit)	
SS-Wirtschafts- und Verwaltungshauptamt	(Gruppe Bauwesen)	
	(Gruppe Wirtschaftsbetriebe)	
	(Gruppe Landwirtschaftl. Verwaltung)	
	Persönlicher Stab Reichsführer SS (Gruppe Presse und Kriegswirtschaft)	
	Reichssicherheitshauptamt (Gruppe SS- und Polizeiwesen)	

among factory workers who were part-time SS members. The only unit of its kind, its services could be summoned in times of epidemic by any of the NSDAP Gauleiters, and it also co-operated with local officials of the German Labour Front. During the war the Röntgensturmbann was absorbed into the medical branch of the Waffen-SS.

In addition to the Sanitätsstaffel attached to every Sturmbann, each Abschnitt contained at least one Sanitätssturm or medical company. A group of several such Stürme, or a single large Sturm, was often termed a Sanitätsabteilung (medical detachment). These units were referred to by the Roman numeral of the Abschnitt in which they were located.

This table lists all the Allgemeine-SS Oberabschnitte, Abschnitte, Standarten and Specialist Units in 1944, with their titles, numbers and abbreviations. (Reproduced from the SS Dienstaltersliste of 9 November 1944)

The SS-Fliegersturm or SS Flying Company was formed in November 1931 at Munich and remained active until absorbed by the DLV, the forerunner of the Luftwaffe, in 1933. By that time there were several SS-Fliegerstaffeln. They were responsible for flying Hitler and other senior Nazis around Germany, during the formative period of the Third Reich.

What amounted to a military police force for the Allgemeine-SS was brought into being in 1935 with the creation of the SS Streifendienst or patrol service. Its functions were policing the SS contingents at party rallies, checking SS documentation at transit points and the like, and rooting out any petty criminal elements in the organisation. Streifendienst units were fairly small and mobile, and their members were specially selected from amongst the most reliable SS men. Whilst on duty they wore a gorget bearing the legend 'SS Streifendienst'.

ᛋᛋ-Oberabschnitte

Name		Location
Nordost		Königsberg
Ostsee		Stettin
Spree		Berlin
Elbe		Dresden
Südwest		Stuttgart
West		Düsseldorf
Süd		München
Südost		Breslau
Fulda-Werra		Arolsen
Nordsee		Hamburg
Mitte		Braunschweig
Rhein-Westmark		Wiesbaden
Main		Nürnberg
Donau		Wien
Alpenland		Salzburg
Weichsel		Danzig
Warthe		Posen
Nordwest		Den Haag
Nord		Oslo
Ost		Krakau
Böhmen-Mähren		Prag
Ostland		Riga
Ukraine		

ᛋᛋ-Abschnitte

No.	Abbr.	Location
I	S	München
II	E	Dresden
III	Sp.	Berlin
IV	Mi.	Hannover
V	W	Duisburg
VI	SO	Breslau
VII	NO	Königsberg
VIII	D	Linz
IX	Ma.	Würzburg
X	SW	Stuttgart
XI	RW	Koblenz
XII	Sp.	Frankfurt (Oder)
XIII	OS	Stettin
XIV	NS	Oldenburg
XV	NS	Hamburg-Altona
XVI	Mi.	Dessau
XVII	W	Münster
XVIII	E	Halle (Saale)
XIX	SW	Karlsruhe
XX	NS	Kiel
XXI	SO	Hirschberg
XXII	NO	Allenstein
XXIII	Sp.	Berlin
XXIV	SO	Oppeln
XXV	W	Dortmund
XXVI	Wei.	Zoppot
XXVII	FW	Weimar
XXVIII	Ma.	Bayreuth
XXIX	SW	Konstanz
XXX	RW	Frankfurt (Main)
XXXI	D	Wien
XXXII	S	Augsburg
XXXIII	OS	Schwerin
XXXIV	RW	Saarbrücken
XXXV	A	Graz
XXXVI	A	Salzburg
XXXVII	BM	Reichenberg
XXXVIII	BM	Karlsbad
XXXIX	BM	Brünn
XXXX	Wei.	Bromberg
XXXXI	Wei.	Thorn
XXXXII	Wa.	Gnesen
XXXXIII	Wa.	Litzmannstadt
XXXXIV	NO	Gumbinnen
XXXXV	SW	Straßburg

ᛋᛋ-Standarten

No.	Abbr.	Location
1.	S	München
2.	RW	Frankfurt (Main)
3.	Ma.	Nürnberg
4.	NS	Altona
5.	RW	Luxemburg
6.	Sp.	Berlin
7.	E	Plauen
8.	SO	Hirschberg
9.	OS	Stettin
10.	RW	Kaiserslautern
11.	D	Wien
12.	Mi.	Hannover
13.	SW	Stuttgart
14.	FW	Gotha
15.	Sp.	Neuruppin
16.	SO	Breslau
17.	NS	Celle
18.	NO	Königsberg
19.	W	Münster
20.	W	Düsseldorf
21.	Mi.	Magdeburg
22.	OS	Schwerin
23.	SO	Beuthen
24.	NS	Oldenburg
25.	W	Essen
26.	E	Halle (Saale)
27.	Sp.	Frankfurt (Oder)
28.	NS	Hamburg
29.	S	Lindau
30.	W	Bochum
31.	Ma.	Landshut
32.	RW	Heidelberg
33.	RW	Darmstadt
34.	S	Weilheim
35.	FW	Kassel
36.	Wei.	Danzig
37.	D	Linz
38.	A	Graz
39.	OS	Köslin
40.	NS	Kiel
41.	Ma.	Bayreuth
42.	Sp.	Berlin
43.	SO	Frankenstein
44.	Sp.	Eberswalde
45.	SO	Oppeln
46.	E	Dresden
47.	FW	Jena
48.	E	Leipzig
49.	Mi.	Braunschweig
50.	NS	Flensburg
51.	Mi.	Göttingen
52.	D	Krems
53.	NS	Heide
54.	Sp.	Landsberg (Warthe)
55.	NS	Lüneburg
56.	Ma.	Bamberg
57.	FW	Meiningen
58.	W	Köln
59.	Mi.	Dessau
60.	NO	Insterburg
61.	NO	Allenstein
62.	SW	Karlsruhe
63.	SW	Tübingen
64.	Wei.	Berent
65.	SW	Freiburg (Br.)
66.	NO	Bartenstein
67.	FW	Erfurt
68.	Ma.	Regensburg
69.	W	Hagen (W.)
70.	SO	Glogau
71.	Wei.	Elbing
72.	W	Detmold
73.	Ma.	Ansbach
74.	OS	Greifswald
75.	Sp.	Berlin
76.	A	Salzburg
77.	OS	Schneidemühl
78.	RW	Wiesbaden
79.	SW	Ulm
80.	Sp.	Berlin
81.	Ma.	Würzburg
82.	W	Bielefeld
83.	RW	Gießen
84.	E	Chemnitz
85.	RW	Saarbrücken
86.	SW	Offenburg
87.	—	Innsbruck
88.	NS	Bremen
89.	D	Wien
90.	A	Klagenfurt
91.	E	Wittenberg
92.	S	Ingolstadt
93.	RW	Koblenz
94.	A	Leoben
95.	BM	Trautenau
96.	BM	Brüx
97.	BM	Eger
98.	BM	Mährisch Schönberg
99.	D	Znaim
100.	BM	Reichenberg
101.	BM	Saaz
102.	BM	Jägerndorf
103.	BM	Aussig
104.	BM	Troppau
105.	NO	Memel
106.	S	Augsburg
107.	BM	Brünn
108.	BM	Prag
109.	Wa.	Posen
110.	Wa.	Hohensalza
111.	Wa.	Kolmar
112.	Wa.	Litzmannstadt
113.	Wa.	Kalisch
114.	Wa.	Leßlau
115.	NO	Zichenau
116.	Wei.	Bromberg
117.	Wei.	Konitz
118.	Wei.	Pr. Stargard
119.	Wei.	Graudenz
120.	Wei.	Kulm
121.	Wei.	Strasburg
122.	SW	Straßburg
123.	SW	Kolmar
124.	SO	Scharley
125.	RW	Metz
	A	Marburg/Drau

ᛋᛋ-Reiterstandarten

No.	Abbr.	Location
R 1	NO	Insterburg
R 2	Wei.	Danzig
R 3	NO	Treuburg
R 4	NS	Hamburg
R 5	OS	Stettin
R 6	W	Düsseldorf
R 7	Sp.	Berlin
R 8	W	Pelkum
R 9	NS	Bremen
R 10	FW	Arolsen
R 11	SO	Breslau
R 12	OS	Schwerin
R 13	RW	Frankfurt (Main)
R 14	SW	Stuttgart
R 15	S	München
R 16	E	Dresden
R 17	Ma.	Regensburg
R 18	D	Wien
R 19	Wei.	
R 20	NO	Tilsit
R 21	Mi.	Hannover
R 22	Wa.	Posen

ᛋᛋ-Nachrichteneinheiten

No.	Abbr.	Location
Na.1	S	München
Na.2	SW	Stuttgart
Na.3	FW	Arolsen
Na.4	W	Düsseldorf
Na.5	Mi.	Braunschweig
Na.6	NS	Hamburg
Na.7	NO	Königsberg
Na.8	Sp.	Berlin
Na.9	E	Dresden
Na.10	SO	Breslau
Na.11	Ma.	Nürnberg
Na.12	OS	Stettin
Na.13	RW	Wiesbaden
Na.14	D	Wien
Na.16	Wei.	Danzig
Na.17	Wa.	Posen
Na.19	BM	Prag

ᛋᛋ-Pioniereinheiten

No.	Abbr.	Location
Pi.1	S	München
Pi.2	SW	Stuttgart
Pi.3	FW	Arolsen
Pi.4	W	Köln
Pi.5	NS	Harburg-Wilhelmsburg
Pi.6	OS	Stettin
Pi.7	NO	Königsberg
Pi.8	Sp.	Berlin
Pi.9	E	Dresden
Pi.10	SO	Breslau
Pi.12	Mi.	Magdeburg
Pi.13	RW	Frankfurt (Main)/Ludwigshafen/Weilburg
Pi.14	D	Wien
Pi.15	A	Salzburg
Pi.16	Wei.	Danzig

ᛋᛋ-Kraftfahrstürme

No.	Abbr.	Location
K.1	S	München/Augsburg
K.2	FW	Erfurt
K.3	Sp.	Berlin/Senftenberg
K.4	NS	Hamburg/Kiel/Bremen
K.5	W	Düsseldorf/Buer (W.)/Dortmund
K.6	E	Dresden/Chemnitz
K.7	NO	Königsberg
K.8	D	Linz/Wien
K.9	SO	Breslau
K.10	SW	Stuttgart/Karlsruhe/Freiburg (Br.)
K.11	Mi.	Magdeburg/Hannover
K.12	Ma.	Bamberg/Schweinfurt/Nürnberg
K.13	OS	Schwerin/Stettin
K.14	RW	Frankfurt (Main)/Wiesbaden-Biebrich/Pirmasens
K.15	A	Graz/Innsbruck
K.16	Wei.	Danzig/Elbing
K.17	NS	Posen/Litzmannstadt
K.19	BM	Asch/Reichenberg/Brünn

Other SS formations

In addition to the regular and specialist SS units, and the first-line reserve of those between the ages of 35 and 45, each Oberabschnitt also contained an independent Stammabteilung or Supplementary Reserve Detachment composed partly of unfit or older men over the age of 45, and partly of younger men whose duties to the State or Party debarred them from taking an active part in the SS. For example, it was customary for full-time regular Police officers to be assigned to a Stammabteilung upon receiving their SS membership. The Stammabteilung carried the name of the corresponding Oberabschnitt and was divided into Bezirke or sub-districts, each Bezirk working in conjunction with a Standarte and bearing the Arabic numeral of the latter. As their title indicated, these additional second-line reservists supplemented the rest of the Allgemeine-SS in the various functions where normal duty personnel and first-line reserves might be overstretched, as in the case of large national parades or celebrations. They were readily distinguishable by the reverse colour scheme employed on their uniform insignia, i.e. a light-grey background to collar patches and cuff titles with black or silver numbers and script. For a short time members of the Stammabteilungen also wore light-grey rather than black borders on their armbands.

During the war SS Helferinnen, or female SS auxiliaries, were recruited to replace male SS personnel who were more urgently needed at the front. Enrolment was on a voluntary basis, and applicants had to undergo a thorough medical examination and background investigation. Helferinnen were trained as teleprinter operators, telephonists and wireless operators, and were assigned to various SS headquarters in Germany and the occupied territories.

Not all who desired to do so could become members of the SS, but those who wished to stand well with the new elite and who could afford to pay for the privilege were allowed to become Fördernde Mitglieder (FM), or Patron Members. All 'aryan' Germans were eligible for FM membership, and those accepted bound themselves to pay a monthly contribution to SS funds. In return they received a badge, a paybook and the goodwill of Himmler's men. In effect, the FM organisation became a sort of 'Old Boys Network' through which members could secure business deals, promotion or employment, and in the Third Reich it virtually replaced the outlawed Society of Freemasons. Membership peaked at 1,000,000 in 1943.

SS SYMBOLISM

'The two Sig-Runes stand for the name of our SS. The Swastika and the Hagall-Rune represent our unshakable faith in the ultimate victory of our philosophy.'
H. Himmler

The Death's Head

Of all SS uniform trappings and accoutrements, the one emblem which endured throughout the history of the organisation and became firmly associated with it was the death's head or *Totenkopf*. It has often been assumed that the death's head was adopted simply to strike terror into the hearts of those who saw it. In fact, it was chosen as a direct and emotional link with the past, and in particular with the elite military units of the Imperial Reich. Medieval German literature and romantic poems were filled with references to dark forces and the symbols of death and destruction, a typical example being the following short excerpt from an epic work by the 15th-century writer Garnier von Susteren:

> 'Behold the knight
> In solemn black manner,
> With a skull on his crest
> And blood on his banner . . .'

In 1740, a jawless death's head with the bones lying behind the skull, embroidered in silver bullion, adorned the black funeral trappings of the Prussian king, Friedrich Wilhelm I. In his memory the Leib-Husaren Regiments Nos. 1 and 2, elite Prussian Royal Bodyguard units which were formed the following year, took black as the colour of their uniforms and wore a massive Totenkopf of similar design on their *Pelzmützen* or busbies. The State of Brunswick followed suit in 1809, when the death's head was adopted by its Hussar Regiment No. 17 and the third battalion of Infantry Regiment No. 92. The Brunswick Totenkopf differed slightly in design from the Prussian one, with the skull facing forward and situated directly above the crossed bones.

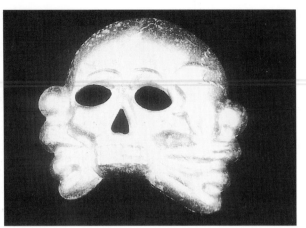

▲ Prussian-style death's head, adopted by the Stosstrupp Adolf Hitler in 1923 and worn by the SS until 1934. These badges were usually made from silver-plated steel or bronze. Modern copies in aluminium circulate widely. (Lumsden Collection)

▶ 1934-pattern SS death's head. This particular example was produced by Deschler of Munich, who made many NSDAP badges and awards. (Lumsden Collection)

During World War I the death's head was chosen as a formation symbol by a number of crack German army units, particularly the stormtroops, flame-thrower detachments and tank battalions. Several pilots, including the air ace Leutnant Georg von Hantelmann, also used variants of it as personal emblems. Almost immediately after the end of hostilities in 1918 the death's head appeared again, this time painted on the helmets and vehicles of some of the most famous Freikorps. Because of its association with these formations it became symbolic not only of wartime daring and self-sacrifice but also of postwar traditionalism, anti-Liberalism and anti-Bolshevism. Nationalist ex-servicemen even had death's head rings, cuff links, tie pins and other adornments privately made for wear with their civilian clothes.

It is not surprising, therefore, that members of the Stosstrupp Adolf Hitler eagerly took the Toten-kopf as their distinctive emblem in 1923, initially acquiring a small stock of appropriate army surplus cap badges. Their successors in the SS thereafter contracted the firm of Deschler in Munich to restrike large quantities of the Prussian-style jawless death's head, which they used on their headgear for the next 11 years. As Hitler's personal guards they liked to

model themselves on the Imperial Bodyguard Hussars, who had become known as the 'Schwarze Totenkopfhusaren' or 'Black Death's Head Hussars', and were fond of singing their old regimental song with its emotive verse:

'In black we are dressed,
In blood we are drenched,
Death's head on our helmets.
Hurrah! Hurrah!
We stand unshaken!'

When, in 1934, the Prussian-style Totenkopf began to be used as an elite badge by the new army Panzer units (which were, after all, the natural successors to the Imperial cavalry regiments), the SS devised its own unique pattern of grinning death's head, with lower jaw, which it wore thereafter.

The 1934-pattern SS Totenkopf ultimately took various forms—right-facing, left-facing and front-facing—and appeared on the cloth headgear of all SS members and on the tunics and vehicles of the SS-Totenkopfverbände and Waffen-SS Totenkopf-Division. It was the centrepiece of the SS Death's Head Ring, and could be seen on dagger and gorget chains, mess jackets, flags, standards, drum covers, trumpet banners and the SS and Police Guerrilla Warfare Badge. Moreover, because of its direct associations with Danzig, where the Prussian Leib-Husaren Regiments had been garrisoned until 1918, it was selected as the special formation badge of the SS-Heimwehr Danzig and the Danzig Police and Fire Service. Himmler wanted his men to be proud of their heritage, and there is no doubt that the honourable military associations of the German Death's Head were well used to that end. It became an instant status symbol in the Third Reich, and an inspiration to those who were granted the privilege of wearing it.

It is worth mentioning that the Totenkopf was also borne by several Wehrmacht elements such as the 5th Cavalry Regiment, the 17th Infantry Regiment, the naval Küstenschutz Danzig, and the Luftwaffe's Schleppgruppe 4 and Kampfgruppe 54 during World War II. (Moreover, many elite units of other nations have likewise used the death's head emblem at various times. These include the British Royal Navy submarine service and 17th Lancers, Mussolini's bodyguard, certain US special forces, imperial Russian cossacks, Polish tank crews, Finnish cavalry and the French security police, to name but a few. Bulgaria even had a Military Order for Bravery in World War I which was graded 'With Skulls'.)

The Runes

Alongside the Totenkopf, the SS-Runen or SS runes represented the elitism and brotherly comradeship of the organisation, and were consciously elevated to an almost holy status. Indeed, as SS men marched off to war in 1939 they sang their battle-hymn 'We Are All SS' ('SS Wir Alle'), which included the line 'We all stand ready for battle, inspired by runes and death's head' ('Wir alle stehen zum Kampf bereit, wenn Runen und Totenkopf führen').

The word 'rune' derives from the Old Norse 'run', meaning 'secret script'. Runes were characters which formed the alphabets used by the Germanic tribes of pre-Christian Europe for both magical and ordinary writing. There were three major branches of the runic alphabet and a number of minor variants, and some runes doubled as symbols representative of human traits or ideals, much as the Romans used oak and laurel leaves to denote strength and victory. In AD 98, in his work *Germania*, the historian Tacitus described in detail how the Germans engaged in

SS belt buckle for enlisted ranks, introduced at the end of 1931. Note the SS motto. This style of buckle remained in use until 1945. (Lumsden Collection)

divination by runes. In the 19th and early 20th centuries runes began to be re-examined by the fashionable 'Völkisch' or 'folk' movements of northern Europe, which promoted interest in traditional myths, beliefs and festivals. Among these groups was the Thule Society; and through his association with its activities during 1919–20 Heinrich Himmler began to look back to the mystical Dark Ages for much of his inspiration. He had always had a fascination for cryptic codes and hidden messages, so it was doubly appropriate that he should tap many of the ideas in pagan symbolism and adopt, or adapt, certain runes for use by his SS.

All pre-1939 Allgemeine-SS recruits were instructed in runic symbolism as part of their probationary training. By 1945, 14 main varieties of rune were in use by the SS, and these are described from A to N below and shown in the accompanying illustrations.

(A) The Hakenkreuz

The Hakenkreuz or swastika was the pagan Germanic sign of the thundergod Donner or Thor. During the 19th century it came to be regarded as symbolic of nationalism and the racial struggle, and in the post-1918 period was adopted by several Freikorps units, primarily the Ehrhardt Brigade. As the senior badge of the Nazi Party and State, it inevitably featured on many SS accoutrements, either static (i.e. standing flat) or mobile (i.e. standing on one point to give the appearance of an advancing movement). An elongated version of the mobile swastika was used by the Germanic-SS in Flanders.

(B) The Sonnenrad

The Sonnenrad or 'sunwheel' swastika was the Old Norse representation of the sun, and was taken up as an emblem by the Thule Society. It was later used as a sign by the Waffen-SS divisions 'Wiking' and 'Nordland', many of whose members were Scandinavian nationals, and also by the Schalburg Corps, which was in effect the Danish branch of the Allgemeine-SS.

(C) The Sig-Rune

The Sig-Rune, also known as the Siegrune, was symbolic of victory. In 1933 SS-Sturmhauptführer Walter Heck, a graphic designer employed by the badge manufacturing firm of Ferdinand Hoffstätter in Bonn, drew two Sig-Runes side by side and thus created the ubiquitous 'SS-Runes' insignia used thereafter by all branches of the organisation. (The SS paid him 2.50 Reichsmarks for the rights to his design!) Heck was likewise responsible for the 'SA-Runes' badge, which combined a runic 'S' with a Gothic 'A'.

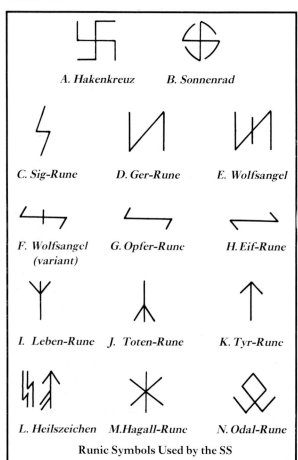

A. Hakenkreuz   B. Sonnenrad

C. Sig-Rune   D. Ger-Rune   E. Wolfsangel

F. Wolfsangel   G. Opfer-Rune   H. Eif-Rune
(variant)

I. Leben-Rune   J. Toten-Rune   K. Tyr-Rune

L. Heilszeichen   M. Hagall-Rune   N. Odal-Rune

Runic Symbols Used by the SS

(D) The Ger-Rune

The Ger-Rune was symbolic of communal spirit, and featured as a variant divisional sign of the Waffen-SS division 'Nordland'.

(E) The Wolfsangel

The Wolfsangel or 'wolf hook' was originally a pagan device which supposedly possessed the magical power to ward off werewolves. It then became a heraldic symbol representing a wolf trap, and as such appeared, and still features, on the coat-of-arms of the city of Wolfstein. During the 15th century it was adopted as an emblem by peasants in their revolt against the mercenaries of the German princes. It was thereafter regarded as being symbolic of liberty and independence, although it was also known as the 'Zeichen der Willkür' or 'badge of wanton tyranny' during the Thirty Years' War. The Wolfsangel was an early emblem of the NSDAP, and was later used as a sign by the Waffen-SS division 'Das Reich'.

(F) The Wolfsangel (variant)

A squat version of the Wolfsangel was the badge of the WA (Weer Afdeelingen), the Dutch Nazi Party's equivalent of the German SA, and was also used by the Germanic-SS in the Netherlands. It was later adopted by the Waffen-SS division 'Landstorm Nederland', which comprised Dutch volunteers.

(G) The Opfer-Rune

The Opfer-Rune symbolised self-sacrifice. It was used after 1918 by the Stahlhelm war veterans' association and was later the badge which commemorated the Nazi martyrs of the 1923 Munich Putsch. It also formed part of the design of the SA Sports Badge for War Wounded, which could be won by disabled SS ex-servicemen.

(H) The Eif-Rune

The Eif-Rune represented zeal and enthusiasm. It was the early insignia of specially selected SS adjutants assigned personally to Hitler and, as such, was worn by Rudolf Hess in 1929.

(I) The Leben-Rune

The Leben-Rune or 'life' rune symbolised life and was adopted by the SS Lebensborn Society and Ahnenerbe. It likewise featured on SS documents and grave markers to show date of birth.

(J) The Toten-Rune

The Toten-Rune or 'death' rune represented death, and was used on documents and grave markers to show date of death.

(K) The Tyr-Rune

The Tyr-Rune, also known as the Kampf-Rune or 'battle' rune, was the pagan Germanic sign of Tyr, the god of war, and was symbolic of leadership in battle. It was commonly used by the SS as a grave marker, replacing the Christian cross. A Tyr-Rune worn on the upper left arm indicated graduation from the SA-Reichsführerschule, which trained SS officers until 1934. It was later the specialist badge of the SS Recruiting & Training Department, and an emblem of the Waffen-SS division '30 Januar', which comprised staff and pupils from various SS training schools.

(L) The Heilszeichen

The Heilszeichen or 'prosperity' symbols represented success and good fortune, and appeared on the SS death's head ring.

(M) The Hagall-Rune

The Hagall-Rune stood for unshakable faith (in Nazi philosophy), as expected of all SS members. It featured on the SS death's head ring as well as on ceremonial accoutrements used at SS weddings.

(N) The Odal-Rune

The Odal-Rune symbolised kinship and family and the bringing together of people of similar blood. It was the badge of the SS Rasse- und Siedlungshauptamt, and emblem of the Waffen-SS division 'Prinz Eugen', the first SS unit recruited from the Volksdeutsche community.

The finer symbolic points of these runes were never generally appreciated by the majority of men who wore them, as instruction in their meaning ceased around 1940.

UNIFORMS AND INSIGNIA

The earliest Nazis wore normal civilian clothing and were distinguished only by their crudely hand-made *Kampfbinde*, or swastika armbands, worn on the left upper arm. With the advent of the paramilitary SA in 1921, however, it became necessary to evolve a uniform specifically for its members. At first their dress lacked any consistency and was characteristically Freikorps in style, generally taking the form of

1932-pattern SS service tunic of a drummer of the 88th SS Fuss-Standarte, c.1935. Note 'swallows nests' and the Honour Chevron of the Old Guard on the right sleeve. The decorations indicate extensive World War I service, in particular the Turkish War Star suggesting participation in the Gallipoli campaign. (Lumsden Collection)

field-grey army surplus or windcheater jackets, waist belts with cross-straps, grey trousers, trench boots, steel helmets and mountain caps. Many SA men simply retained the uniforms they had worn during the 1914–18 war, stripped of badges. The swastika armband was the only constant feature, sometimes bearing a metal numeral or emblem to indicate unit identity, and a metal 'pip' or cloth stripes to denote rank. In 1923 members of the Stabswache and Stosstrupp Adolf Hitler wore similar garb with the addition of a Prussian-style death's head on the cap, usually surmounted by the 'Reichskokarde', a circular metal cockade in the Imperial colours of black, white and red. After the failure of the Munich Putsch and the banning of the SA and the Stosstrupp, the men continued to wear their old uniforms as mem-

Styles of Allgemeine-SS
Uniform
From left to right:
(i) Standard 1932-pattern
black service and parade
uniform for SS-
Oberscharführer.
(ii) Traditional uniform
for SS-Unterscharführer.
This was the first
formalised SS uniform,
worn by all ranks until
1932–34 and donned on
selected ceremonial
occasions thereafter by
members of the Old
Guard.
(iii) Service uniform with
overcoat for SS-
Rottenführer.
(iv)Walking-out uniform
with raincoat for SS-
Sturmbannführer.
(Reproduced from the
Organisationsbuch der
NSDAP, 1937 edition)

bers of the clandestine Frontbanne, adding a steel helmet badge to the centre of the swastika armband.

At the end of 1924 Leutnant Gerhard Rossbach, formerly one of the most famous of the Freikorps and SA leaders, acquired a bargain lot of surplus German army tropical brown shirts in Austria. When the NSDAP was reconstituted and the SA reactivated in February 1925, Hitler kitted his men out with these readily available shirts and had ties, breeches and kepis made to match. Thus, by chance circumstances rather than design, brown became the adopted colour of the SA and the Nazi Party in general.

When the Stosstrupp was re-formed in April of the same year, under the auspices of the SA, its members too were issued with brown shirts. To distinguish them from the SA proper, however, they retained their death's heads and wore black kepis, black ties, black breeches and black borders to the swastika armband. By 9 November 1925, when the term Schutzstaffel was adopted, the brown shirt with black accoutrements was firmly established as the 'traditional uniform' of the SS. The vast majority of SS men, who were also members of the NSDAP, wore the Nazi Party badge on their ties.

On 9 November 1926 the rapidly expanding SA introduced collar patches or *Kragenspiegel* to indicate unit and rank, replacing the badges and stripes formerly worn on the armband. The right patch bore unit numerals and the left patch a Stahlhelm-style system of rank pips, bars and oakleaves. By contrasting the colour of the patch with that of the numerals, an attempt was made to reflect the State colours of the district in which the unit concerned was located, e.g. Berlin SA men wore black and white patches, Hamburg SA men red and white, Munich men blue and white, and so on. This arrangement proved difficult to sustain and the colour combinations ultimately underwent a number of changes. SA unit patches were particularly complex, accommodating not only Standarte, specialist and staff appointments, but also Sturmbann and Sturm designations. (See MAA 220, *The SA 1921–45*.)

In August 1929, the SS likewise introduced collar patches to denote rank and unit. As with the SA, rank was shown on the left patch, or both patches for Standartenführer and above, with unit markings on the right patch. However, the SS system was much more simplified than that of the SA. All SS collar patches were black in colour with white, silver or grey numerals, pips, bars and oakleaves.

Moreover, the unit collar patches were restricted to indicating Standarte, specialist or staff appointment.

To show Sturmbann and Sturm membership the SS devised their own complicated system of 'cuff titles', narrow black bands worn on the lower left sleeve. Within every Fuss-Standarte, each Sturmbann was assigned a colour which bordered the upper and lower edges of the cuff title. The prescribed Sturmbann colours were: Sturmbann I—green; II—dark blue; III—red; IV (Reserve)—light blue. The number and, if appropriate, honour name of the wearer's Sturm appeared embroidered in grey or silver thread on the title. Thus a member of the 2nd Sturm, 1st Sturmbann, 41st SS Fuss-Standarte would wear a green-bordered cuff title bearing the numeral '2', in conjunction with the number '41' on his right collar patch. A man in the 11th Sturm 'Adolf Höh', 3rd Sturmbann, 30th SS Fuss-Standarte would sport a red-edged cuff title with the legend 'II Adolf Höh', and regimental numeral '30' on the right collar patch.

All members of Allgemeine-SS cavalry units had yellow-edged cuff titles, while those of signals and pioneer formations had their titles bordered in brown and black, respectively. A relatively small number of cuff titles bore Roman numerals or designations relating to staff or specialist appointments.

During the autumn of 1929, at the same time as the new SS collar patches and cuff titles were being manufactured and distributed, a small sharp-winged eagle and swastika badge, or *Hoheitsabzeichen*, was introduced for wear on the SA and SS kepi in place of the Reichskokarde. SS bandsmen's uniforms were further modified by the addition of black and white military-style 'swallows' nests' worn at the shoulder.

At the end of 1931 the SS adopted the motto 'Meine Ehre heisst Treue' ('My Honour is Loyalty') following upon a well-publicised open letter which Hitler had sent to Kurt Daluege, commander of the Berlin SS, after the Stennes Revolt, declaring in his praise: 'SS Mann, deine Ehre heisst Treue'. Almost immediately, a belt buckle incorporating the motto into its design was commissioned and produced by the Overhoff firm of Lüdenscheid to replace the SA buckle hitherto worn by all members of the SS. The new buckle was circular in form for officers and rectangular for lower ranks, and continued in wear unchanged until 1945.

In May 1933 shoulder straps or *Achselstücke* were devised for wear on the right shoulder only. These straps were adornments to be used in conjunction with the collar insignia already in existence and indicated rank level (i.e. enlisted man or NCO/junior officer/intermediate officer/senior officer) rather than actual rank.

In February 1934 a silver Honour Chevron for the Old Guard (Ehrenwinkel für Alte Kämpfer) was authorised for wear on the upper right arm by all

Protected by SS men, NSDAP Treasurer Franz Xaver Schwarz (left, in overcoat) watches a parade in his home town of Günzburg, September 1929. Himmler stands nearest the camera. His kepi features the recently introduced eagle and swastika, and his position of seniority is indicated solely by the three white stripes on his SS armband.

SS men at Hamburg Railway Station, c.1934–35. The SS uniform was by now fairly standardised. Runic collar patches worn by men on the left of each row denote membership of the Leibstandarte-SS 'Adolf Hitler'. The others are Allgemeine-SS. (IWM)

members of the SS who had joined the SS, NSDAP or any of the other Party-affiliated organisations prior to 30 January 1933. Qualification was later extended to include former members of the police, armed forces or Stahlhelm who fulfilled certain conditions and transferred into the SS.

The traditional brownshirt uniform of the SS therefore developed almost continually over 11 years and incorporated many additions or alterations at specific times. These can be of great assistance in dating period photographs. With the advent of the black uniform the traditional uniform was gradually phased out, and it was not generally worn after 1934, except on special ceremonial occasions by members of the SS Old Guard.

The Black Uniform

A major change to SS uniform was made in 1932, in response to a government demand that the SA and SS should adopt a more 'respectable' outfit as a condition of the lifting of a ban on political uniforms. On 7 July that year a black tunic and peaked cap, harking back to the garb of the Imperial Leib-Husaren, were introduced for the SS to replace the brown shirt and kepi. These items were made available first to officers, then to lower ranks, and were worn side-by-side with the traditional uniform during 1933 while all mem-

bers were being kitted out. By mid-1934 sufficient quantities of the black uniform had been manufactured for it to be in general use.

The new SS uniform was designed by SS-Oberführer Professor Karl Diebitsch, in conjunction with Walter Heck, who devised the SS-Runes emblem. The tunic comprised a standard four-pocket military-style jacket, the lower two pockets being of the slanted 'slash' type, with a four-button front. There were two belt hooks at the sides and two false buttons at the rear to support the leather waist belt. Insignia were the same as those created for the traditional uniform, and the tunic was worn over a plain brown shirt. The new SS peaked caps were again military in appearance, silver-piped for generals and white-piped for others, with velvet bands and silver cap cords for officers and cloth bands and leather chin straps for lower ranks. As with the kepi, a 1929-pattern eagle was worn above a Prussian-style death's head on the cap. Several minor variants of the black uniform were produced in 1933, including types with three buttons down the front and box-pleated pockets in the tunic 'skirt'; but the whole outfit was formalised and standardised by mid-1934, when the new SS-style *Totenkopf* with lower jaw was introduced.

During the remainder of the 1930s the black service uniform was developed as the SS organisation expanded. Items of clothing began to bear the inspection and production stamps of the SS clothing works and RZM makers, examples being 'VA' (the SS-Verwaltungsamt or Administrative HQ), 'Beste Massarbeit' (best quality mass production), 'Vom Reichsführer-SS befohlene Ausführung' (made in accordance with the instructions of the Reichsführer-SS) and 'RZM M1/52' (the code used by the firm of Deschler on their SS cap badges). Greatcoats were produced; and a series of specialist arm diamonds or *Ärmelraute* devised for wear on the lower left sleeve. Imperial-style 'pork-pie' field caps (known as '*Krätzchen*' or 'scratchers' because of their rough texture), forage caps and steel helmets began to be worn from 1934 on military manoeuvres, at drill training and during guard duty.

On 21 June 1936 a new and larger SS cap eagle replaced the old 1929 pattern, at the same time as the introduction of a series of SS swords and the SS chained dagger. Also around that period, white shirts were authorised for wear under the black tunic on ceremonial occasions. For evening functions such as parties, dances and so on there were black mess jackets for officers and white 'monkey suits' for waiters, all sporting full SS insignia. Finally, as from 27 June 1939, officers were provided with an all-white version of the service uniform for walking-out during the summer period, officially defined as running from 1 April to 30 September each year. The white uniform was also extended to other ranks, but, with the exception of cavalry troopers, was seldom worn.

(It is worth mentioning at this point that every type of SS uniform item has been reproduced for sale to collectors. These fakes, some of which date from the early 1950s, range from the ludicrously poor in quality to the exquisite. Many are now nearly 40 years old, so have an 'aged' look about them. Anyone tempted to buy SS regalia should arm themselves with a large number of good reference books first lest they be defrauded. One particularly good set of cap badges to avoid are the eagles and death's heads marked 'RZM 360/42 SS'—made in Austria in 1980, they are now pinned to many SS caps.)

Full-time SS men were regularly issued with items of uniform and equipment. So far as part-timers were concerned, however, all uniform articles had to be purchased by the SS members themselves at their own expense. The only exceptions were free replacements for items lost or damaged during the course of duty. If an SS man wished to acquire a new tunic, for example, he could either buy it direct from a tailoring shop that was an approved sales outlet of the RZM, i.e. an authorised dealer in Nazi Party uniforms and equipment, or else place a pre-paid order with his local Trupp or Sturm which would, in turn, arrange to requisition a tunic on his behalf from one of the clothing stores run by the SS administrative authorities. The latter regularly produced price lists which were circulated to all SS formations for the attention of would-be buyers.

The gradual introduction of the grey service uniform, combined with the sudden reduction in the number of active part-time Allgemeine-SS men because of enhanced conscription at the outbreak of war, led to a surplus of black uniforms building up in SS stores after 1939. In 1942 the Police collected most of the unwanted black Allgemeine-SS uniforms in Germany and sent them east to the Baltic States,

Hand-embroidered collar patch worn by members of the 88th SS Fuss-Standarte, based at Bremen. (Lumsden Collection)

Poland and the Ukraine for distribution to the native auxiliary police units being raised there. All SS insignia were removed, green facings added, and new badges stitched in place. The remainder of the surplus black uniforms in Germany were shipped west and issued to the Germanic-SS in Flanders, Holland, Norway and Denmark, who again attached their own insignia. Consequently, very few black Allgemeine-SS tunics survived the war with their original German badges intact.

The Grey Uniform

From 1935, field-grey uniforms in the same style as the black service uniform were issued to members of the Leibstandarte-SS 'Adolf Hitler' and SS-Verfügungstruppe for wear during their everyday duties. Simultaneously, an earth-brown uniform of identical cut was authorised for SS-Totenkopf-verbände men serving in concentration camps. The new uniforms immediately proved to be eminently suited to the nature of the tasks performed by these full-time militarised units. Thereafter, members of the Leibstandarte, SS-VT and SS-TV donned the black uniform only on ceremonial occasions and for walking-out.

In 1938 the Allgemeine-SS followed suit by introducing a very elegant pale grey uniform for its full-time staff, thus bringing the whole SS organisation into line with the general war footing of the other uniformed services. The new outfit was identical in style to the black uniform, but bore an SS-pattern shoulder strap on the left shoulder as well as one on the right, and replaced the swastika armband with a cloth version of the 1936-pattern SS eagle. The idea was to give the appearance of a military rather than political uniform, so lending some authority to full-time Allgemeine-SS officers, who were, by the nature of their employment, exempt from service in the Wehrmacht.

The pale grey uniform was issued first to Hauptamt personnel and thereafter to others qualified to wear it. During the war it was gradually superseded by a Waffen-SS style field-grey version, particularly favoured by the SD and senior Allgemeine-SS officers stationed in the occupied territories.

Throughout the war, the 40,000 or so active part-time members of the Allgemeine-SS, who were almost exclusively engaged in reserved occupations,

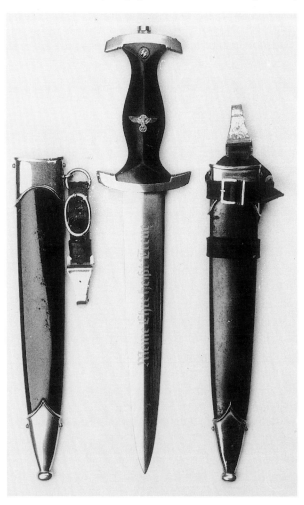

were never issued with grey outfits and so continued to proudly wear the black uniform whilst on duty in Germany. By 1944, however, that most impressive of all uniforms, which had been such a status symbol in the pre-war days, had become an object of derision since its wearers were increasingly thought of as shirking military service. The German civil population revered the Waffen-SS, whom they affectionately dubbed the 'White SS', because of their front-line sacrifices, and despised the part-timers, the so-called 'Black SS'. The grey uniform fulfilled its function by providing the full-time and senior Allgemeine-SS membership with a shield, albeit a psychological one, against such criticism: in the eyes of the public, they were 'White SS'.

Daggers and Swords

The SS service dagger, or *Dienstdolch*, was introduced along with its SA counterpart by the interim Chief of Staff of the SA and Himmler's then superior, Obergruppenführer von Krausser, under SA Order No. 1734/33 of 15 December 1933. Black and silver in colour, it bore the SS motto on the blade and runes and eagle on the grip, and its general design was based on that of a style of 15th–17th century Swiss and German sidearms, usually referred to today as the 'Holbein' style. Worn by all ranks of the Allgemeine-SS with service and walking out dress, the SS dagger was presented to its owner at the special ceremony held when he graduated from SS-Anwärter to SS-Mann. It was not issued at any other time, or en masse like the daggers of the plebian SA. Each SS-Anwärter paid the full cost of his dagger, usually in small instalments, prior to its presentation.

On 17 February 1934 SS-Gruppenführer Kurt Wittje, Chief of the SS-Amt, forerunner of the SS-Hauptamt, forbade the private purchase or 'trading-in' of SS daggers on the open market. Henceforth, daggers could only be ordered from manufacturers through the SS-Amt, for issue via the three main SS uniform distribution centres at Munich, Dresden and Berlin, which regularly processed requisitions received from the various Oberabschnitte Headquarters. Moreover, it was made a disciplinary offence for an SS man to dispose of or lose his dagger, on the

1933-pattern SS dagger, showing the single strap hanger (left) and the   *vertical hanger. (Lumsden Collection)*

1: Trooper, Freikorps Hacketau; Spring 1919
2: Squad leader, Stosstrupp Adolf Hitler, 1923
3: SS-Mann, 1925

A

1: Reichsführer der SS, Heinrich Himmler, 1932
2: Ritter v. Schleich; SS-Fliegerstaffel Süd, 1932
3: SS-Sturmführer, auxiliary police duties, 1933

B

1: SS-Scharführer drummer, Nürnberg SS Standarte, 1933
2: Blood Banner bearer; Nürnberg Rally, 1935
3: SS-Oberscharführer, SS-Streifendienst, c.1936

C

1: Reichsführer-SS Heinrich Himmler, 1937
2: Unterscharführer, Stammabteilung, c.1938
3: SS-Rottenführer, SS-Reiterstandarte 6, Summer 1939

D

1: SS-Gruppenführer Schaub; France, June 1940
2: Ehrenführer Dr. Lammers, 1942
3: SS-Standartenführer; evening dress 1944

E

1: Senior NCO, Security Police, c.1943
2: Oberwachtmeister, SS-Police Regt., 1944
3: Major, Lutftschutzpolizei, c.1944

F

1: Schaarleider, Germaansche-SS in Vlaanderen
2: Opperstormleider, Germaansche-SS en Nederland
3: Rodefører, Germanske-SS Norge, 1944

G

1: Schalburgmand, Schalburg Corps; Denmark, 1944
2: SS-Obergruppenführer Hanke; Breslau, April 1945
3: Volkssturm NCO, Spring 1945

H

grounds that it was a symbol of his office. In that way it was assured that no unauthorised person could buy or otherwise acquire an SS dagger.

As of 25 January 1935, members dismissed from the SS had to surrender their daggers, even though they were personal property paid for by their own means. In cases of voluntary resignation or normal retirement, however, daggers could be retained and the person in question was given a certificate stating that he was entitled to possess the dagger.

Only the finest makers of edged weapons were contracted to produce the 1933-pattern SS dagger. These included Böker & Co., Carl Eickhorn, Gottlieb Hammesfahr, Richard Herder, Jacobs & Co., Robert Klaas, Ernst Pack & Söhne, and C. Bertram Reinhardt. The earliest pieces from the 1933–35 period featured the maker's trademark on the blade, a dark blue-black anodised steel scabbard, and nickel-silver fittings, with the crossguard reverse stamped 'I', 'II', or 'III' to denote that the dagger had passed inspection at the main SS uniform distribution centre responsible for issuing it, viz. Munich, Dresden or Berlin repectively. During 1936–37 makers' marks were replaced by RZM code numbers, scabbards began to be finished with black paint, and the stamped inspection numerals were discontinued as the RZM had by then taken over entirely the regulation of quality control. Finally, from 1938, nickel-silver gave way to cheaper plated steel for the mounts and aluminium for the grip eagle. Despite the declining standard of materials used, a high-quality appearance was maintained and the daggers were consistent in their fine finish.

The SS dagger was suspended at an angle from a single leather strap until November 1934, when Himmler introduced a vertical hanger for wear with service dress during crowd control. However, the vertical hanger, while more stable, was too reminiscent of the humble bayonet frog, and in 1936 the single strap was reintroduced for both walking out and service uniforms; thereafter the vertical hanger was restricted to use on route marches and military exercises.

In September 1940, due to national economies,

the 1933-pattern dagger was withdrawn from production for the duration of the war.

A more ornate SS dagger, to be worn only by officers and those Old Guard NCOs and other ranks who had joined the organisation prior to 30 January 1933, was introduced by Himmler on 21 June 1936. Generally known as the 'chained dagger', it was very similar to the 1933 pattern but was suspended by means of linked octagonal plates, ornately embossed with death's heads and SS runes, and featured a central scabbard mount decorated with swastikas. During the 1936–37 period these chains and fittings, which were designed by Karl Diebitsch, were made from nickel-silver. Later examples were in nickel-plated steel, with slightly smaller, less oval-shaped skulls. Chained daggers bore no makers' marks and it is likely that only one firm, probably Carl Eickhorn, was contracted to produce them.

1936-pattern chained SS dagger, with regulation portepee knot authorised in 1943 for wear by officers of the Waffen-SS, Sipo and SD. (Lumsden Collection)

Each chained dagger had to be privately purchased from the SS administrative authorities in Berlin via the various Oberabschnitte headquarters, requisition forms being submitted regularly at the start of every month. Direct orders from individual officers were not entertained. In 1943, members of the security police and the SD were permitted to wear a knot with the chained dagger when it was being worn with field-grey uniform, and thus the SD became the only branch of the Allgemeine-SS to sport dagger knots. Production of the chained dagger was discontinued at the end of 1943 because of material shortages, and its wear was subsequently forbidden for the duration of the war.

In addition to the standard 1933-pattern and 1936-pattern SS daggers, several special presentation variants were also produced. The first of these was the so-called Röhm SS Honour Dagger, 9,900 of which were distributed in February 1934 by SA Stabschef Ernst Röhm to members of the SS Old Guard. It took the form of a basic 1933-pattern dagger with the addition of the dedication 'In herzlicher Kameradschaft, Ernst Röhm' ('In heartfelt comradeship, Ernst Röhm') etched on the reverse side of the blade. Following the Night of the Long Knives, 200 similar daggers, etched 'In herzlicher Kameradschaft, H. Himmler' were presented by the Reichsführer to SS personnel who had participated in the bloody purge of the SA. A very ornate and expensive SS honour dagger, with oakleaf-decorated crossguards, leather-covered scabbard and Damascus steel blade, was instituted by Himmler in 1936 for award to high-ranking officers in recognition of special achievement. When one was presented to the NSDAP Treasurer, SS-Oberst-Gruppenführer Franz Xaver Schwarz, he responded by secretly commissioning the Eickhorn firm to produce an even more elaborate example, with fittings and chain hanger in solid silver, which he then gave to Himmler as a birthday present.

During the 1933–36 era, SS officers and NCOs engaged in ceremonial duties were permitted to wear a variety of privately purchased army-pattern sabres often with silver rather than regulation gilt fittings. In 1936, however, at the same time as the introduction of the chained dagger, a series of standardised swords in the classic straight-bladed 'Degen' style was created specifically for members of the SS and Police, emphasising the close relationship between the two organisations. There were minor differences between swords for officers and those for NCOs, while SS swords featured runes in their design and Police examples the police eagle on the grip. Personnel attached to SS Reiterstandarten retained the traditional curved sabre for use on horseback.

SS NCOs could readily purchase their swords via local units, from the SS administrative authorities. The officer's sword, on the other hand, which was referred to as the *Ehrendegen des Reichsführers-SS* or Reichsführer's Sword of Honour, was given an elevated status. It was bestowed by Himmler only upon selected Allgemeine-SS commanders and the graduates of the Waffen-SS Junkerschulen at Bad Tölz and Braunschweig. Manufacture of the Ehrendegen ceased in January 1941 for the duration of the war, and SS officers commissioned after that date frequently reverted to the old practice of carrying army sabres.

Still more exclusive were the so-called *Geburtstagsdegen* or 'Birthday Swords', given by Himmler to SS generals and other leading Nazi personalities as birthday presents. They were made to order by Germany's master swordsmith, Paul Müller, who was Director of the SS Damascus Blade School at Dachau, and featured hallmarked silver fittings and blades of the finest Damascus steel with exquisitely raised and gilded dedications from Himmler. Recipients included the German Foreign Minister, SS-Obergruppenführer Joachim von Ribbentrop, and the Führer of Oberabschnitt Nord, Wilhelm Rediess. It was even written into Müller's contract of employment that he could be recalled from leave should

Red-edged cuff title indicating membership of the 12th Sturm, 3rd   *Sturmbann of an SS Fuss-Standarte. (Lumsden Collection)*

Himmler require a birthday sword made at short notice! Their production ceased at the end of 1944.

Decorations

SS men were eligible for the whole range of orders, medals and awards created by the Nazi regime, which recognised both military and civil achievement as well as meritorious service to the NSDAP. Indeed, all SS candidates were expected to win the SA Military Sports Badge and the German National Sports Badge during their probationary training.

In addition to these national honours, a small number of decorations were created specifically for the SS. Foremost among these were the *SS Dienstauszeichnungen* or long-service awards, instituted on 30 January 1938. The series comprised medals for 4 and 8 years' service, and large swastika-shaped 'crosses' for 12 and 25 years. The Dienstauszeichnungen were intended primarily for members of the militarised SS formations, although full-time officials of the Allgemeine-SS were also eligible. Part-time members of the Allgemeine-SS, no matter how long their period of service, fell outside the award criteria and had to settle for one of the succession of NSDAP service decorations. Photographic evidence indicates that the SS Dienstauszeichnungen were not widely distributed and, in fact, it is likely that presentations ceased around 1941, for the duration of the war. Himmler appears to have been virtually the only senior SS leader to wear his decoration consistently .

An SS Marksmanship Badge was created prior to the outbreak of the war, for proficiency in rifle and machine-gun shooting; however, there is no evidence that the badge was put into production. Examples that exist in private collections, bearing the marks of the Gahr firm, are thought to be fakes.

A Silver Clasp for Female SS Auxiliaries was instituted in July 1943 but, again, was never manufactured during the war. Copies in a flat grey metal, with 'SS Helfen' on the obverse and '800' silver stamps and serial numbers in the 600–700 range on the reverse, have been circulating on the collectors' market since 1987.

The Death's Head Ring

One of the most obscure yet potent of all SS uniform accoutrements was the *Totenkopfring der SS*, or SS Death's Head Ring, instituted by Himmler on 10

An SS reservist poses proudly with his son. Note deep turnback cuffs, and 'Reserve' cuff title. The piped trousers and shoes were worn when walking out off duty. (IWM)

April 1934. The Totenkopfring was not classed as a national decoration as it was in the gift of the Reichsführer. However, it ranked as a senior award within the SS brotherhood, recognising the wearer's personal achievement, devotion to duty, and loyalty to Hitler and his ideals. The story of the death's head ring gives an interesting insight into the general workings and philosophy of Himmler and the SS.

The concept and runic form of the ring was undoubtedly adopted by Himmler from Pagan Germanic mythology, which related how the great god Thor possessed a pure silver ring on which people could take oaths (much as Christians swear on the Bible), and how binding treaties were carved in runes on Wotan's spear. The death's head ring comprised a massive band of oakleaves deeply embossed with a Totenkopf and a number of symbolic runes. Each

The SS Death's Head Ring. Struck in solid silver, very few of these survived the War. (Lumsden Collection)

piece was cast, then exquisitely hand-finished by specially commissioned jewellers working for the firm of Otto Gahr in Munich (which also made the 'Deutschland Erwache' standard tops for the NSDAP). The ring started off as a strip of silver which was bent circular to the required finger size and then joined at the front. The death's head was formed from a separate piece of silver and was soldered to the front to cover the join. The larger the ring, the larger the space between the death's head and the two adjacent Sig-Runes. Each completed ring was finely engraved inside the band with the letters 'S.lb.' (the abbreviation of 'Seinem lieben' or, roughly, 'To dear ...') followed by the recipient's surname, the date of presentation and a facsimile of Himmler's signature.

Initially, the weighty silver ring was reserved primarily for those Old Guard veterans with SS membership numbers below 5,000; but qualifications for award were gradually extended until, by 1939, virtually all officers with over three years' service were eligible. Award of the ring could be postponed if the prospective holder had been punished for contravention of the SS Penal and Disciplinary Code.

Certified lists of nominees for the ring, together with their finger sizes, were regularly submitted by the SS Abschnitte headquarters to the SS Personalhauptamt in Berlin, which processed the applications and duly awarded rings and accompanying citations on behalf of the Reichsführer-SS. Each citation read as follows:

'I award you the SS Death's Head Ring.

The ring symbolises our loyalty to the Führer, our steadfast obedience and our brotherhood and comradeship.

The Death's Head reminds us that we should be ready at any time to lay down our lives for the good of the Germanic people.

The runes diametrically opposite the Death's Head are symbols from our past of the prosperity which we will restore through National Socialism.

The two Sig-Runes stand for the name of our SS.

The swastika and the Hagall-Rune represent our unshakable faith in the ultimate victory of our philosophy.

The ring is wreathed in oak, the traditional German leaf.

The Death's Head Ring cannot be bought or sold and must never fall into the hands of those not entitled to wear it.

When you leave the SS, or when you die, the ring must be returned to the Reichsführer-SS.

The unauthorised acquisition of duplicates of the ring is forbidden and punishable by Law.

Wear the ring with honour!

H. HIMMLER'

The ring, which was to be worn only on the ring finger of the left hand, was bestowed on set SS promotion dates. All awards were recorded in the Dienstaltersliste, or Officers' Seniority List, and the personnel files of the holders. All ring holders who were demoted, suspended or dismissed from the SS or who resigned or retired, had to return their rings and citations to the SS Personalhauptamt. Those later accepted back into the organisation would again qualify for the ring. When a serving ring holder died his relatives could retain his citation as a keepsake but had to return his ring to the SS Personalhauptamt which arranged for its preservation in Himmler's castle at Wewelsburg in permanent commemoration of the holder. Similarly, if a ring holder fighting with the Wehrmacht or Waffen-SS was killed in action, his ring had to be retrieved from the body by members of his unit and returned by the unit commander to the SS Personalhauptamt for preservation. In effect, the returned rings of dead SS men constituted military memorials and were cared for as such at Wewelsburg's ever-growing 'Schrein des Inhaber des Totenkopfringes' or 'Shrine to Holders of the Death's Head Ring'.

The death's head ring became so sought-after at

honour that many SS and Police men not entitled to wear it had a variety of unofficial 'skull rings' produced in gold and silver by local jewellers and even concentration camp inmates. Others wore their old death's head jewellery which had been popular in the Freikorps days. However, these lacked any runic symbolism and were rather vulgar representations of the real thing.

On 17 October 1944 the Reichsführer-SS cancelled further manufacture and presentation of the Totenkopfring for the duration of the war. In the spring of 1945, on Himmler's orders, all the rings which had been kept in the Shrine were blast-sealed into a mountainside near Wewelsburg, to prevent their capture by the Allies. To this day, they have never been found.

Between 1934 and 1944 around 14,500 rings were awarded. As at 1 January 1945, according to information compiled by the SD, 64% of these had been returned to the SS on the deaths of their holders (i.e. those now buried at Wewelsburg), 10% had been lost on the battlefield, and 26% were either still in the possession of ring holders or otherwise unaccounted for. That would mean that, in theory, about 3,500 rings might have been in circulation at the end of the war. Nevertheless, original death's head rings are very seldom seen today, and the vast majority of those appearing for sale on the collectors' market are fakes. The history of the death's head ring indicates the gravity with which the SS treated their regalia.

Flags and banners

From 4 July 1926 the SS had the distinction of keeping the most revered flag in the Third Reich, the *Blutfahne* or Blood Banner, which had been carried at the head of the Nazi Old Guard during the Munich Putsch when they were fired upon by the police. It was spattered with the gore of those shot during the encounter, and was thereafter considered to be something of a 'holy relic'. SS-Truppführer Jakob Grimminger from the Munich SS detachment, a veteran of the First World War Gallipoli campaign and participant in the 1922 'Battle of Coburg', was accorded the honour of being the first official bearer of the Blood Banner, and retained that position throughout his career. The last public appearance of the Blutfahne was at the funeral of Adolf Wagner, Gauleiter of Munich-Upper Bavaria, in April 1944. By that time Grimminger had attained the rank of SS-Standartenführer, his association with the mystical flag having assured him a steady succession of promotions.

Preceded by their Feldzeichen, officers and men of the 6th SS Fuss-Standarte march through Berlin, 3 April 1938. Note the bandolier and gorget of the standard bearer.

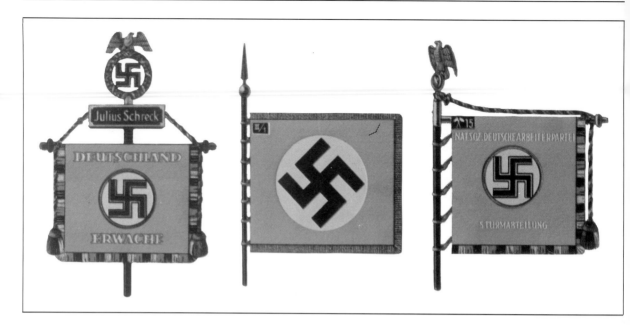

Allgemeine-SS Standards
Left:
The 'Deutschland Erwache' standard, or Feldzeichen, of the 1st SS Fuss-Standarte 'Julius Schreck'.
Centre:
Battalion flag of Sturmbann III of the 1st SS Fuss-Standarte.
Right:
Cavalry standard of the 15th SS Reiterstandarte. (Reproduced from the Organisationsbuch der NSDAP, 1943 edition)

Every Allgemeine-SS Standarte was represented by a banner or *Feldzeichen*, which was itself known as the regimental 'Standarte'. Somewhat reminiscent of the ancient Roman *vexillum* banner, it took the form of a wooden pole surmounted by a metal eagle and wreathed swastika, below which was a black and silver boxed nameplate bearing the title of the SS Standarte on the front and the initials 'NSDAP' on the back. From the box was suspended a red silk flag with a black static swastika on a white circle. The motto 'Deutschland Erwache' ('Germany Awake') was embroidered in bullion on the obverse, with 'Nat. Soz. Deutsche Arbeiterpartei—Sturmabteilung' on the reverse. The flag was finished off with a black/white/red fringe and tassels. Apart from the black name box, the SS Feldzeichen was identical to that of the SA.

When an SS unit achieved roughly regimental proportions it was awarded a Feldzeichen, in a mass pseudo-religious ceremony which took place each September as part of the annual NSDAP celebrations at Nürnberg. During the proceedings Hitler would present many new standards to regimental comman-ders and touch them with the Blutfahne which Grimminger was carrying alongside, so linking in spirit the most recent SS members with the martyrs of the Munich Putsch.

SS Reiterstandarten carried similar but distinc-tive Feldzeichen which had the 'Deutschland Erwache' flag hanging from a wooden bar fixed at right angles to the standard pole. In place of the name box these cavalry standards featured a black patch, or Fahnenspiegel, on the flag cloth, bearing crossed lances and the unit designation in silver.

Each SS Sturmbann was represented by a *Sturmbannfahne* or battalion flag, which took the form of a brilliant red ground with a large black mobile swastika on a white circular field, with black and silver twisted cord edging. In the upper left corner, or canton, a black Fahnenspiegel was em-broidered in silver thread with the Sturmbann and Standarte numbers in Roman and Arabic numerals respectively. The majority of these SS flags were made by the firm of Fahnen-Hoffmann, Berlin.

SS standard-bearers initally wore a 'heart-shaped' SA-style metal gorget or *Kornet*, dating from 1929, upon which was affixed a gilded eight-pointed sunburst surmounted by a facsimile of the centre-piece of the SA belt buckle. In 1938 a new and unique SS-pattern standard-bearer's gorget appeared, crescent-shaped and featuring a large eagle and swastika and a suspension chain decorated with runes and death's heads. SS flag-bearers also wore a massive bandolier in black, with silver brocade edging.

Command flags, or *Kommandoflaggen*, in the shape of rigid pennants on flag poles, were carried as unit markers at large parades or, in smaller versions, were flown from the mudguards of staff cars and other vehicles. They were square, rectangular or triangular in form depending upon designation, and were made of black and white waterproof cloth with rustproof silver thread. Command flags were usually covered in a transparent celluloid casing during bad weather. Each SS Oberabschnitt was required to keep on hand one official vehicle flag and one command pennant for the Reichsführer-SS, for use in the event of a 'flying visit' by Himmler. Other Kommandoflaggen included those for the Heads of SS Hauptämter, SS Oberabschnitte and Abschnitte commanders, the leaders of Standarten, Reiterstandarten, Sturmbanne, SS stores and Inspectorates, and senior Sponsoring Members.

SS-POLICE

The failure of the Munich Putsch in 1923, which was smashed by the Police rather than the army, brought home to Hitler the fact that unrestricted control of the Police would be an essential element in the successful foundation of a long-term Nazi State. Consequently, the years after 1933 witnessed a concerted effort by the Führer to have his most trusted men nominated to senior Police positions, culminating in the appointment of Himmler as Chief of German Police in June, 1936.

Himmler now began formulating his greatest project, the merger of the SS and Police into a single 'Staatsschutzkorps' or State Protection Corps. This was to be achieved first by reorganisation and then by absorption of Police personnel into the SS. Only the most politically reliable and racially suitable policemen would be accepted into the Black Corps, however, and given SS ranks on a par with their Police status. Successful applicants were normally taken into the SS Stammabteilungen, and were permitted to wear the SS runes embroidered on a patch below the left breast pocket of the Police tunic.

The German Police under Himmler fell into two distinct groupings: the Ordnungspolizei or Orpo, the

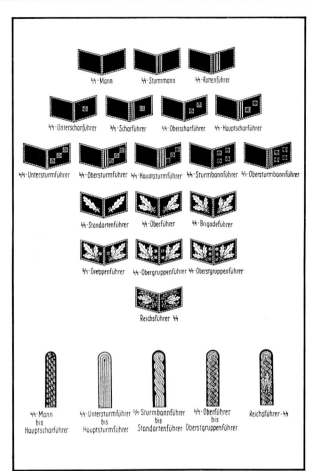

SS Rank Badges, c. April, 1942
This illustration includes the final pattern of collar patches worn by SS and Police Generals, whose badges were altered when the new rank of Oberst-
Gruppenführer was created. Shoulder straps for the Allgemeine-SS are also depicted. (Reproduced from the Organisationsbuch der NSDAP, 1943 edition)

uniformed police; and the Sicherheitspolizei or Sipo, the security police.

The Ordnungspolizei was commanded by SS-Oberst-Gruppenführer Kurt Daluege, and by the end of the war had expanded to include a large number of distinct police formations, each with its own function and its own uniforms.

Prior to September 1939 the security police forces of the Third Reich fell into two distinct groups, those of the Nazi Party and those of the German State. The principal Party force was the *Sicherheitsdienst des RfSS*, or SD, the SS Security Service, which absorbed all other intelligence agencies of the NSDAP in June 1934. The State force

Joachim von Ribbentrop in his uniform as an honorary SS-Brigadeführer, 1936. The Nazi party badge is worn on the tie. The 'dotted' cuff title was a short-lived innovation denoting honorary rank.

was known as the *Sicherheitspolizei*, a general administrative term used to cover both the traditional Kriminalpolizei or Kripo (Criminal Police) and the more recently formed Geheime Staatspolizei or Gestapo (Political Police). In 1939 all of these groups were united to become departments of the Reichssicherheitshauptamt or RSHA, the Reich Central Security Office under Reinhard Heydrich.

The connotations of dread and horror which later attached themselves to the SD in occupied Europe and Russia stemmed from the fact that all members of the security police serving in the conquered territories, whether or not they were members of the SS or SD, were instructed to wear the grey SS uniform with a combination of SD collar and sleeve insignia and Police shoulder straps, to give them the protection of military status yet at the same time distinguish them from other uniformed SS, Police and Wehrmacht personnel. The atrocities carried out by some of these Sipo men, particularly those attached to extermination squads in the East, reflected directly on the SD proper, the majority of whose members were engaged purely on intelligence gathering. In fact, while the death squads which penetrated deep into Soviet territory in 1941 were entitled 'Einsatzgruppen der Sicherheitspolizei und des SD', only 3% of their personnel were SD men. The majority were Waffen-SS (34%), army (28%), and uniformed police (22%), assisted by Gestapo (9%) and Kripo (4%).

During the period 1940–42 a large number of younger members of the Ordnungspolizei, supplemented by Allgemeine-SS conscripts, were transferred to 30 newly created independent Police Regiments comprising around 100 battalions, each of 500 men. They were organised and equipped on a military basis and served as security troops in the occupied countries. In February 1943 these German formations were officially designated SS-Police Regiments, to distinguish them from the recently raised native 'Police Rifle' units; and they subsequently gained a reputation for extreme brutality and fanatical loyalty to Himmler and the Nazi regime. The vast majority were posted to Russia, Eastern Europe and the Balkans, where roaming partisan bands of anything up to brigade strength were causing havoc behind the German lines. Various pro-German local militias and home guard units composed mainly of Balts, Cossacks and Ukrainians were consolidated into an auxiliary police force known as the *Schutzmannschaft* or Schuma. All of these police formations were completely separated from the Wehrmacht, and took their orders from Himmler through his HSSPfs. In effect, they were remote extensions of the Allgemeine-SS operating in the occupied territories. (See MAA 142, *Partisan Warfare 1941–45*, and MAA 169 *Resistance Warfare 1940–45*.)

By 1944, therefore, through his continued absorption of police responsibilities, Himmler had succeeded in achieving ultimate control of all conventional German police forces, the fire brigade, railway and post office guards, rescue and emergency services, intelligence agencies, anti-partisan formations; even night-watchmen. Moreover, all the corresponding domestic police forces in the conquered countries, including even the English Constabulary serving in the Channel Islands, came under his authority. The active Allgemeine-SS proper was by that time a relatively small organisation it its own right, and numerically far inferior to the Waffen-SS. However, its leaders directed the operations of hundreds of thousands of uniformed and plain-clothes policemen throughout the Greater German Reich, and had access to their intimate local know-ledge. In that way, the often-maligned and faceless bureaucrats of the Allgemeine-SS exercised a power and influence more widespread and effective than anything contemplated by their fighting comrades in the Waffen-SS.

SS 1925-pattern armband. The black borders distinguish it from the general NSDAP version. (Lumsden Collection)

THE GERMANIC-SS

Himmler saw the cornerstone of the Greater German Reich as being an SS organisation with native branches in each of the Western occupied territories. He envisaged the ultimate creation of a new western Germanic state to be called Burgundia, grouping the Netherlands, Belgium and north-east France, which would be policed and governed solely by the SS according to the SS code and would act as a buffer to protect Germany proper from invasion. The general aim was to attract all the Nordic blood of Europe into the SS, so that never again would the Germanic peoples come into mutual conflict.

To that end, Himmler established a replica of the German Allgemeine-SS in Flanders in September 1940. This *Allgemeene-SS Vlaanderen* was joined two months later by the Dutch *Nederlandsche-SS* and in May 1941 the *Norges-SS* was formed in Norway. Members of these organisations retained their own languages and customs, and came under the jurisdic-tion of their own national pro-German political leaders. In the autumn of 1942, however, these formations were amalgamated to become branches of a new all-embracing Germanic-SS under Himmler's direct orders. They were retitled *Germaansche-SS in Vlaanderen, Germaansche-SS en Nederland* and *Germanske-SS Norge*. After the raising in April 1943 of the Danish *Germansk Korpset*, later called the Schalburg Corps, the Germanic-SS was complete, with a total active membership of almost 9,000 men. Their primary wartime task was to support the local

police by rooting out partisans, subversives and other anti-Nazi elements.

The black uniform of the Germanic-SS in Flanders was virtually identical to that of the Allgemeine-SS. The only points of difference were that the peaked cap featured a large elongated swastika instead of the SS eagle, and a black diamond bearing the SS runes was worn on the left upper arm instead of the swastika armband. Rank insignia was worn on the left collar patch like that of the Allgemeine-SS, while the right collar patch was blank. On the lower left sleeve a black and silver cuff title bore the legend 'SS-Vlaanderen', and the belt buckle featured SS runes in a circle of oakleaves. In civilian clothes, members of the Germanic-SS in Flanders could wear a circular lapel badge with a white swastika on a black background, while Patron Members had their own diamond-shaped badge bearing the SS runes and the letters 'B.L.'. Members of the Vlaanderen-Korps, the reserve branch of the Flemish SS, wore a similar uniform but were not entitled to sport the peaked cap or arm diamond; they had forage caps with a silver swastika on the left side, and their cuff titles read 'Vlaanderen-Korps'. Moreover, their belt buckles had only a semi-circle of oakleaves around the runes.

Members of the Germanic-SS in the Nether-lands were similarly attired. A regimental number appeared on the right collar patch, with SS runes on the right upper arm. A triangle bearing a silver Wolfsangel on a red and black background was worn on the left sleeve, and a silver Wolfsangel also appeared on the peaked cap instead of the SS eagle.

All ranks wore a blank cuff title on the lower left sleeve.

The uniform of the Germanic-SS in Norway represented a departure from the norm for the Allgemeine-SS. It consisted of a ski cap, tunic, ski trousers or breeches, and mountain boots. Peaked caps were never worn by the Norwegian SS, and jackboots were seldom seen either. On the left upper arm was worn the so-called 'sun eagle' of Quisling's Norwegian Nazis, in silver and black, above a cuff title bearing the legend 'Germanske-SS Norge'. A silver sunwheel swastika appeared on the right collar patch, with SS runes on the right upper arm.

The Schalburg Corps in Denmark adopted a black uniform conforming with that of the Allgemeine-SS, and rank insignia was again the same although the nomenclature used was that of the Danish police. The main points of difference were that the SS cap eagle was replaced by a winged sunwheel swastika, and a sunwheel swastika also featured on the right collar patch and on the belt buckle. A Danish heraldic shield, comprising three blue lions on a yellow field with red hearts, was worn on the upper left arm above a cuff title bearing the word 'Schalburg'. On ceremonial guard duty, a highly polished black German steel helmet was worn with a large white sunwheel swastika on the right-hand side. For more active purposes, the Corps was armed with light infantry weapons and supplied with a more practical khaki field uniform. A so-called Schalburg Cross bearing the Corps motto 'Troskab vor Aere' ('Our Honour is Loyalty') was instituted late in the war, and at least one posthumous award is recorded. (It is reported that boxes of these crosses were strewn across the street outside the Schalburg Corps HQ at the Freemasons' Lodge in Copenhagen at the end of the war, and were eagerly picked up by passers-by.)

In addition to the regular Germanic-SS formations, the Allgemeine-SS established its own *Germanische Sturmbanne* or Germanic Battalions in the areas of the Reich where there were large concentrations of workers imported from the Nordic countries. These foreigners in Germany numbered several hundred thousand by the end of 1942, and posed a major problem for German internal security. To assist in their control, Flemish and Dutch SS officers and men, most of them fresh from front-line service in Russia, were employed by German firms to engage upon a propaganda campaign in the factories. They succeeded in persuading such a large number of their compatriots to join the local Allgemeine-SS that seven Germanic Battalions were set up in the major industrial areas of Berlin, Brunswick, Dresden, Düsseldorf, Hamburg, Nürnberg and Stuttgart. Service in the Germanische Sturmbanne was voluntary and unpaid, and was performed either after work hours or at weekends. Uniforms were supplied by the Allgemeine-SS, and comprised the standard outfit minus the tunic; insignia were worn on the shirt, in the manner of the old SS Traditional Uniform. It is not known if members were permitted to wear any special badges indicative of their national origin, but it would appear doubtful.

Himmler wearing the grey SS uniform introduced in 1938. Note the two shoulder straps,

Reichsführer-SS collar patches, bullion arm eagle and officer's belt buckle.

THE PLATES

A1: Trooper, Freikorps Hacketau; Remscheid, Spring 1919

Former Freikorps men provided the SS with some of its earliest recruits, and this figure illustrates a typical member of Freikorps Hacketau, which, under the command of Oberstleutnant Menz and Major von Falkenstein, fought hard to defeat the local Communists in Remscheid during the spring of 1919. The trooper has retained his basic army uniform, to which have been added the collar badges and cuff title of his Freikorps. The death's head, roughly hand-painted on the steel helmet, was adopted by several independent Freikorps units and became an emblem of traditionalism and anti-Bolshevism in Germany during the immediate post-World War I period. As such, it was eagerly adopted by the infant SS.

A2: Squad leader, Stosstrupp Adolf Hitler; Bayreuth, 1923

This illustration depicts Karl Fiehler, one of the founder members of the Stosstrupp Adolf Hitler, carrying the Imperial War Flag as he appeared at the 'German Day' rally in Bayreuth on 2 September 1923. His uniform is basically Reichswehr in character, but features an early hand-made Kampfbinde of the NSDAP on the left sleeve, and a Prussian-style Totenkopf and national cockade on the Austrian army-pattern cap. Although the Stosstrupp had no formalised rank structure, a white stripe to the armband denoted the wearer's general position as a squad leader. Fiehler participated in the ill-fated Munich Putsch on 9 November 1923, for which he was imprisoned; he later became lord mayor of the city and an SS-Obergruppenführer during the Third Reich.

A3: SS-Mann, 1925

By the end of 1925, SS men were wearing the recently adopted plain brown shirt uniform of the SA, but with several distinctive accoutrements. The SS was now set apart not only by the Totenkopf but also by black kepis, black ties, black borders to the swastika armband and, more gradually, black breeches. The truncheon was frequently used against political opponents in the street battles of the time.

B1: Reichsführer der SS, Heinrich Himmler, 1932

In 1932 Heinrich Himmler held the rank of SS-Gruppenführer, and although he was titular Reichsführer der SS he was still very much subordinate to the SA Stabschef, Ernst Röhm. Here he wears the collar patches of his rank, the SS officer's belt buckle created in 1931, and the newly introduced cuff title for departmental heads. The badge on the left breast pocket commemorates his participation in the Fourth Party Rally held at Nürnberg on 1–4 August 1929. Note also the small NSDAP eagle, introduced in 1929 to replace the national cockade on the kepi.

B2: Staffelführer Ritter von Schleich; SS-Fliegerstaffel Süd, 1932

Seen here in his rather 'personalised' version of the newly introduced black SS service uniform, Eduard

Himmler in conversation with Honorary SS-Obergruppenführer Dr. Hans Lammers, who is wearing the white summer tunic. Both sport the Golden Party Badge. Lammers' field cap is non-regulation.

Ritter von Schleich led SS-Fliegerstaffel Süd during its short existence. Throughout the First World War Eduard Schleich was a professional army pilot, and by the end of 1917 had scored 25 victories as the Staffelführer of Jagdstaffel 21, receiving the 'Pour le Mérite' Order on 4 December. On 6 July 1918 he was decorated with the Knight's Cross of the Bavarian Military Max-Joseph Order, a rare honour which enabled him to adopt the title 'Ritter von'. The so-called 'Black Knight of Germany' ended the war with a tally of 35 Allied aircraft.

Note the strangely placed collar patches, the SA/SS Pilot's Wings over the right breast pocket, the prized Military Max-Joseph Order hanging from the left lapel, the non-regulation belt and cross-strap, and the lack of any armband or cuff title.

B3: SS-Sturmführer, auxiliary police duties, 1933

In February 1933 over 15,000 SS men were issued with firearms and given police powers to arrest left-wing opponents. This SS-Sturmführer wears the formalised traditional uniform, with the black and silver twisted piping sported by junior officers during this period, and is distinguished as an auxiliary policeman solely by the 'Hilfspolizei' armband worn over the SS brassard. The heavy leather gauntlets were issued to dog handlers.

C1: SS-Scharführer drummer, Nürnberg SS Standarte, 1933

Each SS Sturmbann had a *Spielmannzug* or fife and drum corps, and this drummer is attached to the 2nd Sturmbann of the Nürnberg SS Standarte. The

'swallows' nests' were peculiar to musicians, and dated from 1929. The strap on the right shoulder had just been introduced, and the black mourning band was worn over the standard SS brassard while attending funerals, remembrance days and similar events. During the period 1932–34, when the black service uniform was in course of manufacture and distribution, it was not uncommon for SS men to mix newly issued items with old ones. This Scharführer has acquired a peaked cap, but still wears his traditional brown shirt pending the issue of the new black tunic. The decoration on the left breast is the so-called 'Deutsches Feldehrenzeichen', one of a series of unofficial First World War commemorative awards prohibited from further wear at the end of 1935.

C2: Blood Banner bearer; Nürnberg Rally, 1935

From 4 July 1926 the SS had the honour of guarding the most revered flag of the NSDAP, the *Blutfahne* or 'Blood Banner', which had been carried at the head of the Nazi old guard during the Munich Putsch and was spattered with the blood of those shot in the encounter. Jakob Grimminger of the Munich SS detachment was the first official bearer of the Blood Banner, a position he retained until the collapse of the Third Reich. He is depicted here as he appeared at the Party Rally at Nürnberg in 1935, with the new helmet decals introduced for that event. The standard bearer's gorget is of the SA pattern, and decorations include the Blood Order, the Golden Party Badge, the Coburg Badge, and the Turkish War Star 1915, referred to by the Germans as the 'Iron Crescent' since it was the Turkish equivalent of the Iron Cross. Grimminger's blank right collar patch and 'Süd' cuff title indicate his membership of the staff of SS Oberabschnitt Süd.

C3: SS-Oberscharführer, SS-Streifendienst, c.1936

From 1935, each SS Oberabschnitt commander could form a Streifendienst as and when required, from his most reliable men, to patrol areas tempo-

NCOs of the Sipo and SD uncovering a cache of hidden weapons in Warsaw, November 1939. Security policemen usually operated in civilian clothing, and there were occasions when they were 'mistaken' for resistance fighters and shot. The field grey uniform gave some degree of protection.

▲ *Badge worn by Patron Members of the Germanic-SS in Flanders. (Lumsden Collection)*

▶ *Wolfsangel insignia worn by members of the Germanic-SS in the Netherlands. (Lumsden Collection)*

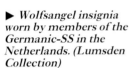

rarily out of bounds to SS personnel or to police the SS contingents at Party rallies. During the annual 9 November celebrations in Munich, for example, only selected SS men in possession of specially issued passes valid for the day could enter the restricted area where Hitler and his hierarchy congregated. It was the Streifendienst who checked these passes and ensured that no unauthorised SS 'spectators' slipped through. All members of a Streife wore a nickel-plated gorget bearing the legend 'SS Streifendienst'. This Oberscharführer, in standard service dress, also wears the 1933-pattern SS dagger in its vertical hanger, and the SA Military Sports Badge and German National Sports Badge are pinned to his left breast pocket. Note too the 1934-pattern death's head and 1936-pattern SS eagle on the peaked cap.

D1: Reichsführer-SS Heinrich Himmler, 1937

SS officers had the option of purchasing leather overcoats for winter wear. Himmler very much favoured them, and could often be seen in one, sporting the distinctive collar patches of his rank and the silver-grey lapels worn by Oberführer and above. A 1936-pattern SS chained dagger hangs from his belt, as does the holster for a Walther PPK—after 1933 Himmler always carried a pistol for personal protection. Here he is collecting for the Winter

Charities Campaign, or Winterhilfswerk, which was organised on an annual basis by the Nazi People's Welfare Organisation, headed by SS-Gruppenführer Erich Hilgenfeldt.

D2: SS-Unterscharführer, Stammabteilung; walking-out dress, c.1938

Members of the Stammabteilungen, or Supplementary Reserve Detachments, wore SS uniform with distinctive silver-grey collar patches and cuff titles. This Unterscharführer, a wounded veteran of the First World War, is attached to the 93rd Fuss-Standarte of SS Oberabschnitt 'Rhein-Westmark'. He wears regulation walking-out dress, with long, piped trousers and shoes. White shirts were authorised for formal occasions from about 1936. Since there is no belt with this outfit the dagger is suspended by means of an internal hanger, with the strap attachment extending through a slit below the left pocket flap of the tunic.

D3: SS-Rottenführer, SS-Reiterstandarte 6, Summer 1939

This Rottenführer serving with the 5th Company of the 6th SS Cavalry Regiment (Düsseldorf) wears the white linen summer uniform newly authorised for wear between 1 April and 30 September each year. Crossed lances feature on both the unit collar patch and the specialist sleeve diamond, while the cuff title is edged in distinctive cavalry yellow. A German Horseman's Badge is pinned to the left breast pocket. All members of SS Reiterstandarten were issued with plain-hilted army-pattern sabres, although officers awarded the Ehrendegen usually preferred to wear it when 'walking out'.

E1: SS-Gruppenführer Schaub; France, June 1940

Although technically attached to the Reichsführung-SS, Julius Schaub was Hitler's chief personal adjutant during the war and was never far from his side. Schaub is depicted here as he appeared at the signing of the French armistice in June 1940. The field cap is standard army issue, with an SS Totenkopf pinned over the national cockade. The grey version of the black Allgemeine-SS service tunic, designed to be more military looking, has two shoulder boards instead of one, and a sleeve eagle to replace the

SS-Gruppenführer Reinhard Heydrich at his desk in 1937. Note the single shoulder strap, finely embroidered collar patches, and the bullion cuff title of a Hauptamtschef. The SS Death's Head Ring can clearly be seen on his left hand.

armband. The cuff title on the right sleeve commemorates Schaub's membership of the Stosstrupp Adolf Hitler in 1923, and his Old Guard status is reinforced by the Alte Kämpfer chevron, Coburg Badge, Golden Party Badge and the Blood Order ribbon stitched to the right breast pocket flap.

E2: Ehrenführer Dr. Lammers, 1942
The Head of the Reich Chancellery, Dr. Hans Lammers, was a wily civil service lawyer who had solved many legal tangles for the Nazis during their formative years. He was subsequently rewarded by Himmler with honorary SS rank, and rose to Obergruppenführer on 20 April 1940. As an Ehrenführer he did not have operational authority over any SS forces but, nevertheless, was entitled to sport the insignia and accoutrements of a full SS general. The Reichsführer's Sword of Honour hangs from his left side, and the brocade belt, embroidered with oak-leaves and runes, was worn on ceremonial occasions.

E3: SS-Standartenführer Graf Strachwitz, evening dress, 1944
The aristocratic Hyazinth Graf Strachwitz von Gross Zauche und Camminetz was a Standartenführer attached to the staff of Oberabschnitt Südost, and the first SS member to win the Knight's Cross of the Iron Cross with Oakleaves, Swords and Diamonds. He earned the award in April 1944, while serving as an army (not Waffen-SS) Panzer commander on the Eastern Front. Here he wears the sparkling decoration to good effect with regulation SS evening dress. The jacket sports full insignia, complete with its distinctive breast badge comprising a death's head over a scroll bearing the SS motto, 'Meine Ehre heisst Treue'. The ornate buttons are embossed with SS runes surrounded by a wreath of oakleaves.

F1: Senior NCO, Security Police, c.1943
During the war, members of the Security Police serving in the occupied territories were afforded the protection of the grey uniform of the Sicherheitsdienst, irrespective of whether or not they were members of the SD or, indeed, of the SS. The regulation grey Allgemeine-SS tunic became increasingly difficult to find from 1942 onwards, however, and this senior NCO has had to make do with an army field blouse. The blank right-hand collar patch and the 'SD' sleeve diamond, originally denoting attachment to the old SD-Hauptamt, eventually became universal throughout the Sipo and the SD, while the rank insignia combines the collar patch of an SS-Hauptscharführer with the shoulder straps of a Police Hauptwachtmeister or Kriminaloberassistent. The ribbon of the War Merit Cross 2nd Class, often awarded to the Security Police for their 'special services', extends from the second buttonhole, and this man has also been awarded a Police long-service decoration and the SA Sports Badge in Silver.

F2: Oberwachtmeister, SS-Police Regiment, 1944
From 1943, German Police formations serving as security troops in the occupied territories were known as 'SS-Police' Regiments, to distinguish them from the recently raised native auxiliary 'Police Rifle'

units. This Oberwachtmeister has just been awarded the Iron Cross 2nd Class and the prized Guerrilla Warfare Badge in Bronze. His uniform is that of the civil Schutzpolizei, with a 'Deutsche Wehrmacht' cuff title to show temporary attachment to the armed forces. The silver bullion SS runes below the left breast pocket indicate that the wearer is one of the minority of German policemen who succeeded in gaining full membership of the Allgemeine-SS.

F3: Major, Luftschutzpolizei, c.1944

The Luftschutzpolizei, a highly mobile rescue organisation which rendered immediate help to trapped and injured air-raid victims, was created in May 1942, and placed under the command of Himmler in his capacity as Chief of the German Police. Members were exempt from conscription, so those who were also in the Allgemeine-SS could keep up their normal SS activities. Luftschutzpolizei uniform comprised a curious combination of standard issue Luftwaffe items bearing Police insignia. This Major, whose SS membership is denoted by breast runes, has been awarded the War Merit Cross 1st and 2nd Classes, the Luftschutz Decoration and the German National Sports Badge in Silver. He also wears his basic NSDAP membership badge prominently on the tunic, a fairly common practice amongst the civil Police during wartime.

G1: Schaarleider, Germaansche-SS in Vlaanderen, c.1942

The black uniform of the Flemish SS was virtually identical to that of the German Allgemeine-SS. The only real points of departure were the silver swastika on the cap, the runic patch on the left sleeve, and the distinctive belt buckle. All members wore blank 'unit' collar patches and the standard 'SS-Vlaanderen' cuff title, since no Flemish formation was large enough to justify the production of regimental, battalion or even company insignia.

G2: Opperstormleider, Germaansche-SS en Nederland, c.1943

This Dutch SS Opperstormleider sports the Iron Cross 2nd Class, Infantry Assault Badge and Wound Badge, won while serving with German forces on the Eastern Front. The 'wolf hook' emblem of Mussert's NSB is worn on the peaked cap and the left sleeve, with SS runes on the right sleeve. The cuff title is blank. Unit identity is shown solely by the '3' on the right collar patch, indicating membership of the 3rd Standaard, based at Amsterdam. Note the use of a black shirt, unique to this branch of the SS.

G3: Rodefører, Germanske-SS Norge, 1944

The Germanic-SS in Norway evolved a very distinctive uniform with mountain cap, ski trousers and ankle boots. All ranks wore the sunwheel swastika on the right collar patch, a 'Germanske SS Norge' cuff title, and the so-called 'SS-Solørn' or 'SS sun eagle' on the left sleeve. An SS runes patch appeared on the right arm. This Rodefører has been awarded the Germanic Proficiency Rune in Silver, which can be seen on the left breast pocket. This was the Germanic-SS equivalent of the SA Sports Badge.

H1: Schalburgmand, Schalburg Corps; Denmark, 1944

The Schalburg Corps was, in all but name, the Germanic-SS in Denmark, and the uniform worn by its members reflected that fact. One unique feature, however, was the highly coloured Danish heraldic shield worn on the left sleeve, a concession to the fervently nationalistic outlook of this formation. The sunwheel swastika featured prominently on the right collar patch, the belt buckle and the peaked cap, as well as on the steel helmet, which was issued to men on guard duty. This Schalburgmand, or Private, is equipped with a German Kar .98k rifle and ammunition pouches.

H2: SS-Obergruppenführer Hanke; Breslau, April 1945

On 28 April 1945, Himmler was expelled from the Nazi Party and all his government offices for attempting to negotiate an armistice with the Western Allies. Hitler subsequently appointed Karl Hanke, an Allgemeine-SS Obergruppenführer and Gauleiter of Lower Silesia, as the new Reichsführer-SS, although Hanke had by that time abandoned his post in the besieged city of Breslau and never received word of his promotion. Here Hanke wears a field-grey leather overcoat and field cap, in his capacity as commandant of 'Fortress Breslau'. Around his neck is hung the German Order, the highest decoration of the NSDAP, which he received on 12 April 1945.

H3: Volkssturm NCO, spring 1945

Members of the hastily mustered Volkssturm or Home Guard units which sprang up across Germany at the end of the war were allowed to wear any suitable clothing readily to hand. This former SS-Oberscharführer of the 2nd Reserve Sturm, 42nd SS Fuss-Standarte has utilised his old Allgemeine-SS uniform, with a Luftschutz steel helmet and the obligatory 'Deutscher Volkssturm Wehrmacht' armband. He is heavily armed with an MP40, Panzerfaust anti-tank weapon and a 1943-pattern stick grenade.

INDEX

(References to illustrations are shown in **bold**. Plates are shown with page and caption locators in brackets.)

Abschnitte (Districts) 10, **14**

badges **12**, **13**, **21**, 21, **39**, **45**
  see also insignia; runes; swastikas
banners 37–39 *see also* Blood Banner; standards
belt buckle **17**, 21
Berchtold, Josef **3**, 4
Blood Banner 8, **C2** (27, 44), 37
Brigadeführer **40**

cap, NCO's/man's peaked **7**
cavalry units (Reiterstandarten) 12, **D3** (28, 45), **38**

daggers 24, 24, **33**, 33–35
Death's Head 15–17, **16**
  see also Ring, Death's Head
decorations 35
Denmark, Schalburg Corps **H1** (32, 47), 41, 42
Diebitsch, Oberführer Professor Karl 22, 33
drummers **18**, **C1** (27, 44)

Ehrenführer (Honorary Officers) 8, **E2** (29, 46)

female SS auxiliaries (SS Helferinnen) 15, 35
Fiehler, Karl 4, **A2** (25, 43)
flags 37–39 *see also* Blood Banner; standards
Flemish SS (Germaansche-SS in Vlaanderen) **G1** (31, 47), 41
Freikorps 4, 16, **A1** (25, 43)
Führer des Abschnittes/Oberabschnittes (F. Ab/F Oa) 10
Fuss-Standarten, SS **6**, 12, **23**, **D2** (28, 45), **34**, 37, 38

Germaansche-SS en Nederland **G2** (31, 47), 41–42, **45**
Germaansche-SS in Vlaanderen **G1** (31, 47), 41
Germanic-SS 33, 41–42, **45**
Germanske-SS Norge **G3** (31, 47), 41–42
gorgets 38
Graf, Ulrich 4, 5
Grimminger, SS-Truppführer Jakob **8**, **C2** (27, 44), 37
Gruppenführer **E1** (29, 45–46), **46**

Hanke, SS-Obergruppenführer Karl 8, **H2** (32, 47)
Hauptämpter (departments) 9
Heck, Walter 22
Heydrich, SS-Gruppenführer Reinhard **46**
Hilfspolizei (auxiliary police) **B3** (26, 44)
Himmler, Reichsführer-SS Heinrich 6, 7, **8**, 17, **21**, **B1** (26, 43), **D1** (28, 45), 35, 39, 40–41, **42**, **43**
history, early 3–6
Hitler, Adolf 4–5, 6, 20

insignia 19–24, 33–39, **45**

see also badges; runes; swastikas
armbands 19–20, **41**
collar patches 20–21, **23**
cuff titles 21, **34**
Honour Chevron, Old Guard 21–22
shoulder straps (*Achselstücke*) 21

Klintsch, Leutnant Hans–Ulrich 4
Krausser, Obergruppenführer von 24

Lammers, Ehrenführer Dr. Hans **E2** (29, 46), **43**
Leibstandarte-SS 'Adolf Hitler' 3, 6, **22**
Luftschutzpolizei **F3** (30, 47)

Major, Luftschutzpolizei **F3** (30, 47)
Müller, Paul 34–35
Munich Putsch 4–5, 37

NCOs **F1** (30, 46), **H3** (32, 48), **44**
NSDAP (Nationalsozialistische Deutsche Arbeiterpartei) 4, 5
Netherlands SS
  see Germaansche-SS en Nederland
newspaper, 'Das Schwarze Korps' **9**
Norwegian SS (Germanske-SS Norge) **G3** (31, 47), 41–42
Nürnberg SS Standarte **C1** (27, 44)

Oberabschnitte (Oa. or Regions) 9–10, **14**
Obergruppenführer **H2** (32, 47), **43**
Oberscharführer 14, 20, **C3** (27, 44–45)
Oberwachtmeister, SS-Schutzpolizei (Police Regiment) **F2** (30, 46–47)
Opperstormleider, Germaansche-SS en Nederland **G2** (31, 47)
organisation 9–15, **10**
  regional 9–10, **14**
  unit 10, 12–13

Patron Members (Fördernde Mitglieder – FM) 15
Police Regiment (SS-Schutzpolizei) **F2** (30, 46–47) *see also* Hilfspolizei; SD; SS-Police; Sicherheitspolizei

racial policies 7
ranks 11 *see also* badges
Reichsführer der SS
  see Himmler, Reichsführer-SS Heinrich
Reserve Detachments (Stammabteilung) 15, **D2** (28, 45), **35**
Ribbentrop, SS-Brigadeführer Joachim von **40**
Ring, Death's Head 35–37, **36**, **46**
Ritter von Schleich, Staffelführer Eduard **B2** (26, 43–44)
Rodeförer, Germanske-SS Norge **G3** (31, 47)
Röhm, Ernst 4, 5, 6, 34
Rottenführer 13, **20**, **D3** (28, 45)
runes 17–19, **18**, *see also* badges; insignia

SA (Sturmabteilung) 4, 5, 6
SD (Sicherheitsdienst des RfSS – Security Service) **F1** (30, 46), 39–40, **44**
SS (Schutzstaffel) 5, 6–8
SS-Fliegerstaffel Süd **B2** (26, 43–44)
SS-Mann **4**, 5, **21**, **22**, **A3** (25, 43)
SS-Police 39–41
SS-Totenkopfverbände 3
SS-Verfügungstruppe (SS-VT) 3, **8**
Schaarleider, Germaansche-SS in Vlaanderen **G1** (31, 47)
Schalburg Corps, Denmark **H1** (32, 47), 41, 42
Scharen (sections) 13
Scharführer, drummer, Nürnberg SS Standarte **C1** (27, 44)
Schaub, SS-Gruppenführer Julius 4, **E1** (29, 45–46)
Schreck, Julius 4
Schutzpolizei, SS (Police Regiment) **F2** (30, 46–47)
Schutzstaffel *see* SS
Schwarz, SS-Oberst-Gruppenführer Franz Xaver **21**, 34
Security Service *see* SD
Sicherheitspolizei (Sipo – Security Police) 39, **44**
  see also SD
specialist formations **13**, 13–14, **14**
squad leader, Stosstrupp Adolf Hitler **A2** (25, 43)
Staffelführer, SS-Fliegerstaffel Süd **B2** (26, 43–44)
standards (Feldzeichen) **4**, 6, 37, **38**, 38
  see also banners; Blood Banner
standarten (regiments) 12, **14**
Standartenführer **E3** (29, 46)
Stosstrupp Adolf Hitler 3, 4, **16**, 16, 19, 20, **A2** (25, 43)
Strachwitz, SS-Standartenführer Hyazinth Graf **E3** (29, 46)
Streifendienst (patrol service) 14, **C3** (27, 44–45)
Sturmabteilung (SA) 4, 5, 6
Sturmbanne (battalions) 12–13, 21
Sturmbannführer **20**
Stürme (companies) 13
Sturmführer, auxiliary police duties (Hilfspolizei) **B3** (26, 44)
swastikas 17–18, **18**, **21**, 21
  see also badges, insignia
swords 34–35
symbolism 15–19

trooper, Freikorps Hacketau **A1** (25, 43)

uniforms **18**, 19–24, **20**, 33–39
Unterscharführer **20**, **D2** (28, 45)

Volkssturm **H3** (32, 48)

Wittje, SS-Gruppenführer Kurt 24